FORGIVING
Others

To: DAKota
God Bless YA!!

Jeremiah 33:3

FORGIVING
Others

Keys *to* Healing Deep
Wounds *of* Your Past

LOUIS HUSSER

Trilogy Christian Publishers A Wholly Owned Subsidiary of Trinity Broadcasting Network2442 Michelle Drive Tustin, CA 92780

First Trilogy Christian Publishing paperback edition, December 2018

Trilogy Christian Publishing/ TBN and colophon are trademarks of Trinity Broadcasting Network.

For information about special discounts for bulk purchases, please contact Trilogy Christian Publishing.

Manufactured in the United States of America

10 9 8 7 6 5 4 3 2 1

Library of Congress Cataloging-in-Publication Data is available.

ISBN 978-1-64088-157-0

ISBN 978-1-64088-158-7 (ebook)

Introduction

This is a personal growth book. It is, even more so, a spiritual growth book.

The Bible is the greatest personal/spiritual literature ever written. God's Word has endured for thousands of years and has withstood millions of critics. Timeless personal and spiritual philosophies have been borne from the truths of the Bible while all other philosophies fall by the wayside. God proclaimed His Truths before man ever expounded on them. Within these pages I will attempt to explain these rich truths that will nurture you both spiritually and personally.

Without spiritual growth, our personal growth is only considered to be "behavioral modification". Behavioral modification comes only from the surface of our minds until we are changed deeply within our spirits. Our spirit is who we really are and is where we truly live. Surface changes ebb and flow as all emotions do. Only when we have a spiritual change can we allow our spirits to feed our minds, wills, and emotions.

Our spirit is the only part of us that is eternal. When we die, our soul, (mind, will, and emotions), cease. Shouldn't we place more emphasis on the eternal portion of our being? We are not so much *humans having a spiritual experience*, as we are *spirits having a temporary human experience*. Only after our spirits have changed, can the temporal portion of our being experience genuine change. In order to sustain our positive mental attitudes, we must have an unshakable source of truth and strength. Only within our spirits can we enter into a genuine, eternal relationship with Jesus Christ.

Christ and He alone will become our source of strength. His teachings transform us into new individuals. All other humanistic "self-help" ideas or philosophies are superficial at best. Circumstances, positions, titles, finances, status symbols, or mental and physical health can all change in one day. Life's variables can change us from a positive to a negative person or a negative person into a positive person, relative to our chapter of life.

Henry Ford was asked, "If you lost everything, your entire empire, what would you do?" His response was brilliant. "I'd have it all back tomorrow, because no one can take away the knowledge and drive I have within me!"

When our personal constitution or source of belief is founded on the eternal truths of God's Word, we are unstoppable.

Dedication

The first and foremost dedication of this book is obviously to Jesus Christ: my Lord, my Savior, and my Sustainer. He is the ultimate example of forgiveness.

The second dedication of this book is to my dad, the late Delos Eston Husser; church planter, missionary, and cowboy preacher. It was not until later in my life that I realized the many battles he fought and won! I was somewhat aware of his PTSD from being a Navy Veteran of WWII. Often, I'd call to check on him and he would tell me of his loss of the previous night's sleep due to panic attacks. He referred to them as "war nerves". I would reply with the question, "War nerves or 'pastoral nerves'?"

He faithfully preached the gospel and ministered to people for over 40 years. He never quit – not once. He never took a sabbatical, and as I recall, only took two vacations in his entire lifetime.

He planted and/or revitalized six churches during his life's work, only to receive much criticism from other ministers. Because of his forgiving nature, he did not allow anyone to hinder the work God called him to do.

He took on battles with the local school board over the issue of teaching evolution. He fought battles with city councils for allowing bar rooms to operate within the illegal parameter of his church facility. He never turned a "blind eye" to cultural wrongs and many times positioned himself on the front lines. The word "compromise" was not in his vocabulary. He did not know how to quit or to back down from a challenge. His rough exterior was a reflection of his strong interior and straight laced, core beliefs.

To him, the battles outside of the church were the easier ones. His most difficult battles were with the enemies from within the church, battles with the people of whom he had helped the most, only later to have these people turn against him. *Psalms 55: 12-14 NKJV, "For it is not an enemy who reproaches me; then I could bear it; nor is it one who hates me who has exalted himself against me; then I could hide from him. 13 But it was you, a man my equal, my companion and my acquaintance. 14 We took sweet counsel together and walked to the house of God and the throng."*

Beneath the rough exterior and deeply beneath his even rougher interior, was a layer of compassion for people. He genuinely cared enough to forgive the ones who hurt him the deepest. Not only from his sermons but from his way of life, I learned how to forgive people. I, and countless others, stand on his shoulders. He fought battles we will never face. He pioneered trails of ministry which enables us to walk down freely. We have learned from his struggles and thousands of people have better lives because of his ministry.

Thanks, Dad. I'll see you soon!

Foreword

There are so many things that those of us in the church could do better. There are so many things that those of us in the Body of Christ could do better. It does not matter your age, it does not matter your race, and it does not matter your gender. It does not matter how long you have been in the church; you can be a senior soldier, or you can be a babe in Christ. It does not matter your vocation or your position in the church; you can be a preacher, a deacon, a trustee, an usher, a choir member or a pew member. The fact of the matter is there are a number of things that all of us can do better.

Some things that may come to mind are:

- I can do better at reading my Bible.
- I can do better at sharing my faith.
- I can do better at praying more.
- I can do better with my church attendance.
- I can do better giving my tithes and offerings.

And the list can go on and on, because there are many areas where we as believers, need improvement.

However, even though the above list is needed and necessary for all of us in the church, I still think that there is another topic that should be on our list. That topic is the word FORGIVENESS!

When we think of all the things we have read about, heard about, or have been a part of and could have been avoided if forgiveness would have been applied. When we think about:

- Family members who are not speaking to each other because of unforgiveness;
- Churches who have split because of unforgiveness;
- Former friends who are now enemies because of unforgiveness;
- Couples who are no longer together because of unforgiveness;
- In-laws who have become out-laws because of unforgiveness;

- And all of us know so many other relationships that the enemy has destroyed because of unforgiveness.

There is hope for all of us who struggle with or have been hurt by someone because of unforgiveness. My friend and brother, Pastor Louis Husser's new book, "Forgiving Others", is written to help all of us. From his personal situations as a pastor and community leader, to his many years of counseling others, this book will address all your questions when it comes to forgiving others.

Read this book, apply this book, share this book, so that all of us can benefit when we learn the crucial Biblical principle of "Forgiving Others".

—FRED LUTER JR.
Pastor, Franklin Avenue Baptist Church New Orleans, Louisiana
Former President, Southern Baptist Convention

Acknowledgements

No one is an island. We are hardwired for relationships. Even the Lone Ranger had a Tonto! Loving relationships are vital. We are the average of our five closest friends. Therefore, I am extremely blessed.

I give special thanks and acknowledgement to my wife, Charlotte Johnson Husser, who has been my soul mate since 1975. She has spent many hours working on this project. From correcting my grammar to making sense of my sentences, she has been amazing. Her goal has been for this book to help change the lives of people as its contents have changed her own.

Thanks to my church family, Crossgate Church of Robert, Louisiana, where I have served as senior pastor since 1992. Our deacons and elders have prayed and encouraged me during the writing of this book.

Thanks to Cori Bruno, poet and artist who has worked diligently on the illustrations you will see inside the covers this book.

My prayer warrior friend, Norma Webb, has done a wonderful job on the editing. Appreciation is extended to my niece, Shalayne Walters, for diagrams.

Thanks to my daughter, Leah Danielle Ried, and to Tisha Pol for the talented photography work.

This project is a compilation of years of ministry to our Lord.

Table of Contents

CHAPTER 1
Forgiving Is Not An Option

People are naturally secretive. It is human nature to attempt to hide the undesirable events of our lives. We all have skeletons in the closets of our past so let's cover this in detail.

Matthew 6: 14 – 15 14 NKJV, "For if you forgive men their trespasses, your heavenly Father will also forgive you. 15 But if you do not forgive men their trespasses, neither will your Father forgive your trespasses."

This is part of "The Model Prayer." If your Bible has this labeled as *The Lord's Prayer*, please draw a line through *Lord* and label it as THE MODEL PRAYER. This is not the *Lord's* Prayer. Here Jesus is teaching us to ask for forgiveness. Jesus never sinned; therefore, He doesn't need to repent or to pray for forgiveness. There is a difference. This is the model prayer for you and I to pray. Christ didn't need to ask His Father for some of these things. He *is* all these things in our lives. So now, let's examine it in the proper context. Many of you are familiar with this passage as you learned this as children in religious schools.

Matthew 6: 9 – 13 NKJV, 9 "In this manner, therefore, pray," the pronoun is understood - *you* are to pray this. *"Our Father in heaven, Hallowed be Your name. 10 Your kingdom come. Your will be done on earth as it is in heaven. 11 Give us this day our daily bread. And forgive us our debts as we forgive our debtors. 13 And do not lead us into temptation but deliver us from the evil one. For Yours is the kingdom and the power and the glory forever. Amen."*

Now the prayer stopped with *"Amen"*. Verse 14 is an explanation. Jesus is going to expound on forgiving other people as He mentioned the word *debt*. It's a word that simply means what someone has taken something from you, and you should forgive that person. So, let's begin by discussing the prayer He told us to pray. *"Our Father, in heaven, hallowed be Your name."* He addressed to whom He was writing and to whom He was praying. You and I must make sure that our prayer is not just something we are thinking in our minds, but clearly know *Whom* the object of our prayer is. We must know to Whom we are addressing our petition.

A great example of this is The Tangipahoa Parish School Board, Louisiana, being the object of numerous lawsuits filed by the ACLU. In one suit on school prayer, the ACLU wanted us to compromise on "praying in the name of Jesus." They wanted us to pray a type of generic prayer and address it to no "god" in particular. During deliberations I was asked if this would meet with my approval. I immediately replied, "No, it does not! To pray without directing it to Jesus is like mailing a letter and not putting an address on it. It isn't getting anywhere." How ridiculous! Tangipahoa Parish School Board won this suit, and to this day we still have the privilege to pray in the Name of Jesus.

"Our Father, in heaven, hallowed be Your name." This addresses God with adoration. We are adoring God, calling Him, *Lord*, and saying, "Holy is Your name."

10 *"Your kingdom come. Your will be done on earth as it is in heaven."* This means that we are agreeing with God to have His sovereign will in our lives. "God, I want You to have Your way in this messed-up and mixed-up world". The only thing that is going to sustain us, as a culture here in America, is for us to pray, "God, in spite of the stubborn will of man, would You please have Your way." What this verse means is "God, I am agreeing with you and I relinquish my selfish rights to have everything my own way. I'm fine with it. God, whatever *You* do, I am ok with it."

This verse is a request. God, give us our daily bread. He didn't say, "God, give me enough bread so I will not have to chop wheat again next year." Instead Jesus teaches us to pray, "God, give us our daily bread. Lord, I don't know what I need today because I never know what is about to happen". Our futures are uncertain. God wants us to live by faith in HIM. Trust Him for the outcome of our futures. Our prayer should be, "God, I'm going to trust You today that I will have the health and ability to start my day, get out of bed, and earn a living." If you worry about the future, you will worry it into trouble.

11 "Give us this day our daily bread." Give us what is sufficient for today's needs.

12 "And forgive us our debts, as we forgive our debtors." Debt means we owe something. We have taken something that wasn't ours. The Bible explicitly discourages owing or having debt. Debt will keep you awake at night. It has been said that if I lose my job, in ninety days the car will be repossessed. In 120 days, the furniture will be repossessed. In six months, the house will be history. That should drive you to trust God by faith. No one has job security unless you are a funeral director or a preacher. We are the only professions who have job security. Funeral directors and ministers have *job security*, but we don't necessarily have *income security.* So, He is saying, trust God for today's needs. If we have debts, God will forgive us, but we are also going to reciprocate. Those who owe us, we are going to forgive them. Of all the things He says in this prayer, Jesus paused at the end and expounded on the area of forgiveness. He could have taken four subjects: PRAISE, ADORATION, SURRENDER, AND TRUST, and spoken for hours. However, He struck the Achilles' heel when He insisted on dealing with offenses. In Verses 14 and 15, Jesus could have discussed the points of all other subjects in this prayer. However, when He got to the end and said, "Amen," He said, (paraphrased), "Oh yeah, by the way. That reminds me; let me teach you how to forgive."

14 "For if you forgive men their trespasses, your heavenly Father will also forgive you. 15 But if you do not forgive men their trespasses, neither will your Father forgive your trespasses."

The essence of this book is that there are **nine** Biblical truths or principles that must be put in place when you forgive somebody, or you will have superficial forgiveness. It's going to get deep. It's going to get real. The subtitle of the book is: THE KEY TO HEALING THE DEEP WOUNDS OF YOUR PAST.

Many people have old wounds. They may have verbalized on the surface, "I forgive." Unfortunately, they have not been through the nine Biblical principles that I have discovered in my thirty-five years of counseling and over forty years of extensive study of the Word of God. Many people have not even scratched the surface of understanding those nine principles. They spend their lives in wonder and confusion as to why they are still having issues with relationships.

There are three predominant root problems that cause issues resulting in strained relationships. They are guilt, immorality, and bitterness. I dare say, of the three root problems covered in this book, bitterness is the most prevalent one. Anger is cause by bitterness, and anger is a result of being offended by someone we have never truly forgiven. We *say* we have forgiven them, but more than mere words are required for this to take place. Once I counseled with a gentleman and his ex-wife. They were attempting reconciliation. He was a tough old dude. His biological father abandoned him when he was two years old. I asked how that affected his life, but I already knew the answer. I wondered if *he* knew the answer. It became apparent that he did not. He was very much in denial. He explained the way he coped is by never thinking about it. He had destroyed two marriages, but it never occurred to him that he had never dealt with issues from his dysfunctional childhood. Those deep-rooted issues prevented him from being in a functional marital relationship as an adult. Professional counselors refer to that as *suppression*. Those negative thoughts and hurt feelings had been pushed down very deeply into the subconscious mind. Another word for this is denial. It is no wonder this man was bitter, angry, and hateful to those who are closest to him and incapable of being happily married.

I have had people in my counseling office who have destroyed as many as five marriages! Once a man came into my office for premarital counseling. It was to be his fifth marriage. I asked him to explain what happened to the first one. What happened to the second? What happened to the third? The fourth one? In his opinion, the demise of all four failed marriages was the result of someone else's mistakes. I said, "Sir, I have news for you. I have observed one thing: this many women can't be wrong." I asked him to give me the single common denominator in each of his failed marriages. It got very quiet in those next few moments. (crickets)

I have heard many stories of people who are struggling with relationship issues. We have all been hurt in some way or another. There are women who've been hurt so often by men, they hate all men, all male authority, and ultimately

God Himself. When women have suffered abuse from a man, often they transfer that "finger print" of the abuser to ALL MALES. Then, they are told of a loving, compassionate, Heavenly Father who loves them. Subconsciously, realizing that God is a man, they never comprehend the love of "Abba Father, God". This is a very real and serious stumbling block for many women.

The following is a list of life-altering offenses. If we were in small group setting this list could multiply, because remember, *everything affects us.* Good or bad in some way or another we are directly affected by every event in our lives. There are good experiences in our lives and there are bad experiences; yet all experiences must be learning experiences.

#1. Verbal abuse. If you are a born- again believer, you must learn to put a filter on your mouth and never be verbally abusive. Consequently, most of us have experienced those painful, stinging words of verbal abuse. Those words hurt! The Bible says hurtful words are as puncture wounds. Now, there is a difference in a puncture and a cut. A cut can be superficial, but a puncture wound goes very deep; and treatment is required from the inside out to prevent serious infection. I have been very fortunate over the past twenty-five years to own horses. Only a few of them have had puncture wounds, but when they do, daily treatment is required in order for proper healing to take place. Puncture wounds must be opened at the surface each day, for the healing to take place from the inside first. The same holds true for words of verbal abuse. We must heal from the inside out. Verbal abuse is as painful puncture wounds. *Proverbs 12:18 NKJV, "There is one who speaks like the piercings of a sword, but the tongue of the wise promotes health."*

Psalm 57:4 NKJV, "My soul is among lions; I lie among the sons of men who are set on fire, whose teeth are spears and arrows, and their tongue a sharp sword."

"A torn jacket is soon mended, but hard words bruise the heart of a child," Henry Wadsworth Longfellow.

#2. Emotional neglect. It hurts. The life-altering offense of neglect is often very subtle. I see many children who are being raised with parental neglect as the result of being turned over to a digital screen for their entertainment. Those children do not develop proper communication skills or relational skills due to emotional neglect. We all need eye-to-eye, verbal communication with other human beings. God made us to interact with each other and to interact with Him. Proper human contact is vital for healthy human development.

#3. Abandonment. Someone who should have remained in your life, just walked away. It is painful. Abandoned children go through a list of torturing questions: *Why? What did I do to cause them to leave me? How bad was I to cause them to abandon me? What did I do to cause Mom or Dad to leave?* These questions are counter-productive. These children grow up with major insecurities. They fear the next person they trust will leave them as well. It becomes easier to never trust at all.

#4. Physical abuse. Whether it comes from the hands of a spouse or a parent, physical abuse has results that reach far beyond the scope of its present action. Maybe you were the recipient of someone's uncontrolled anger. Possibly you were physically assaulted. What provokes this violent nature in a person? A significant percentage of all domestic violence calls, responded to by law enforcement officers, have been linked to pornography in the home. Some signs of physical abuse are stuttering, psychosomatic disorders, anxiety, fears, compulsive behavior, poor self-acceptance, over reaction to touch. If you have been the victim of physical abuse, I suggest you check the resources at healthyplace.com.

#5. Sexual abuse. I have listened to countless females and males who were tormented by sexual abuse. Now I dare say, of all the heart-wrenching stories I have heard, the ones concerning sexual abuse are the most life altering. There is an epidemic. It is rampant. I am an old-fashioned guy. When I hear their stories, I cry with those devastated individuals. My first question is, "Did you report this crime to the authorities?" Somebody needs to face judicial punishment. There is no excuse. It does not matter if it was that "strange uncle" in your family. Your strange uncle should be in jail! I am a proponent of the victim. Sexual abuse must stop! I have heard all the excuses. "Well, it would tear up the family." When there is a sexual perpetrator in the family, that family is already torn apart. Forget keeping the skeletons in the closet. Someone must stop perpetrators! Do something! Say something! Don't be a victim of the hurt and keep silent. The situation will only worsen. If not held accountable, the perpetrator will victimize another innocent person. The effects of sexual abuse are too many to list; however, one that concerns me is the fact that the victim often loses his "moral compass". Often, he never learns moral boundaries and could live a promiscuous lifestyle and possibly abuse others. This produces a cycle of behavior that is difficult to break.

 # 6. Financial abuse. Financial abuse is broad. Someone may have stolen your identity. A fraudulent business partner may have victimized you. As a child an older kid who took your lunch money may have bullied you. No matter what the situation, you may have been financially victimized to the point of losing your home, your business, or even resulting in the loss of your family. This causes the pain of insecurity and can develop into greed or hoarding as time progresses.

#7. Church Ministry abuse. *Proverbs 18:19 NKJV, "A brother offended is harder to win than a strong city, and his contentions are like the bars of a castle."*

When I became pastor, I purposed in my heart to love and help people who had been offended from previous church experiences. I wanted to be a part of the healing process by using the Word of God. I wanted to love them and give Biblical instruction, so they would no longer have these strong walls around them. Their contentions are like the bars of a castle, the Bible says. I've got news for you. The love of God and the Word of God are more powerful than any bars of castles and walls that could ever be built by man. God can heal them. Let the journey of healing begin!

#8. Suicide of a loved one. It hurts every day. This pain comes in many forms: loss, guilt, regret, hopelessness, etc. The "ripple" effect of suicide is endless. Not only does it affect immediate family, the loss continues to ripple through several layers of relationships. There is no way to explain exactly how many people are affected by just one suicide. Once I had a gentleman in my office who expressed to me that he had considered ending his life. He said the pain of life was too great and he could no longer bear it. I said, "Let me give you something to think about. You have two children. So, you're telling me you are okay with your two precious children, ages seven and eight, standing at your casket, looking at you in that box, and retaining that picture in their minds for the remainder of their lives? Every day of their lives, that visual picture will haunt them. They will always feel that they were not worthy of your love because *your* pain was too great?" It was a sobering question. Please allow me to interject this statement. When a person is at the point of ending his life, he needs professional, medical help *immediately.* Often times there is an underlying medical issue that needs to be dealt with which is causing these harmful suicidal thoughts. Help is available. Suicide is NEVER the answer. NEVER!

Forgiving is not an option. *Matthew 6: 14 – 15 NKJV, "For if ye forgive men their trespasses, your heavenly Father will also forgive you: But if you do not forgive men their trespasses, neither will your Father forgive your trespasses."* We need to be forgiven. You must realize your need to be forgiven constantly by an Almighty God. He will forgive. However, this forgiveness is conditional. He will not forgive us if we do not forgive others. Here is an absolute. Forgiving our offenders is not an option *if* you want to *be* forgiven. I believe we need to interpret the Scripture literally, within proper context. Look at this verse as literally what Jesus was teaching. He went straight to the point. If you want to be forgiven by a holy God, you must forgive those who have hurt you. Can you imagine having a log jam in your forgiveness and Christ holding all these sins over you because you haven't forgiven your offender?

This is not optional, if you want to be forgiven. *Psalm 66:18 NKJV, "If I regard iniquity in my heart, The Lord will not hear."* What do we learn from this verse? When you and I harbor sin, bitterness, or unforgiveness, God will not hear us. What this verse is saying, God will not honor our praying if we have not extended our forgiveness to others whether they have asked for it or not. Now does God hear every prayer? That is the big question asked many times by those who are beginning to grow in their prayer lives. God will *hear* every prayer because God is omniscient. God knows everything that is going on. He hears everything. There is not a word spoken that does not enter His ear. He hears what we pray.

However, there is a difference between what God hears and what God honors. David says in *Psalm 66:18 NKJV, "If I regard iniquity in my heart"*, (which is the broader word for lifestyle of sin), *"The Lord will not hear."* You may say, "Now, preacher, if that's the case, God has been hearing my prayers but He cannot honor them. I need to get cleaned up before God because I have a backlog of unforgiven sins due to my failure to forgive others." Again, I say, "Forgiveness is not an option." We must forgive people if we want God's forgiveness.

Early in my ministry I spent nine years traveling from coast to coast in music and evangelism. To be honest with you, of the revivals I conducted, I can count on one hand the number of churches that did not experience a great revival. Our evangelistic team recorded nine albums and was privileged to see more than two thousand people surrender their hearts and lives to Christ for salvation. We saw the mighty hand of God in each service. After this, God closed the door for that ministry and I accepted a position at my home church in Franklinton, Louisiana, as youth minister. This was an indescribable experience. I was privileged to see teens become very bold in their faith. Their lives, as well as the lives of their friends, were truly changed for the Lord! We grew from six teens to around fifty teenagers in only six months! This ministry exploded with growth. God did an awesome work in that little church! When I left that ministry and took the position as senior pastor at a church in Shreveport, I was fired up and enthusiastic for the cause of Christ! God had used me in evangelism for nine years, an explosive six months in youth ministry, and now to serve my first church as pastor.

There were underlying, negative issues within the church, but God still moved in a mighty way! We began that pastorate with about forty people. Every Monday night, forty to fifty people, met at the church and went door-to-door, sharing the gospel. The church grew expeditiously. It was unbelievable. We sold old buses that would barely run and purchased much nicer buses. We remodeled the nursery and started new outreach ministries. The church funded several foreign mission projects. Exploding with growth, new families joined almost every week! We had baptismal service almost every Sunday night for twenty-two months. More than 221 people came to Christ and joined our church in those twenty-two months. However, the "old guard" in that church was losing control. I was too young and inexperienced to realize there was a control issue and a power struggle. I questioned, "Why aren't many of our original church members happy with all these new people coming to faith in Christ?" There was only a very small nucleus of the old guard that did not approve of all the changes our church experienced because they had been there so long they felt as though they owned the church. I'm sure you are familiar with that type of people. They had donated money all those years and felt they had seniority to make all decisions concerning the church. Our new members posed a terrible threat to them. Everything I did was heavily criticized by that nucleus of leaders. If there had been texts or social media back then, I would have been "socially crucified"! They despised everything I did.

The church grew rapidly, but so did the contention. I would drain the baptistery each Monday morning then get down on my knees inside the baptistery and pray, "God, You are doing so many great things but *what is happening?*" As a young pastor, my heart was fully devoted to my congregation. I was under the impression everyone should be happy with this success. Finances were increasing. Every area of the church was experiencing rapid growth; but still there was a faction of contention. After much prayer and consultation, I traced the source of the faction back to my associate pastor. Upon the advice of my mentor, I fired that disloyal staff member. When I made that decision, the nucleus began circling the wagon; getting ready for war. They obtained a copy of the church role and made phone calls to dozens of people, most of who had never heard me preach. On a Wednesday night, it was brought to a vote, whether I would stay as pastor or leave. These wicked church leaders, "the old guard," spoke before the congregation and said such things as, "There is nothing wrong with him morally." One of them even said, "You can melt Marilyn Monroe and pour her over him and he wouldn't flinch. He is *that* moral; but I just hate him." Another one said, "There is nothing wrong with him doctrinally; I just don't like him. Someone has got to stop this young man." That night the votes were cast, and I lost the position as senior pastor by a narrow margin of six votes. I was devastated! I remember thinking, "This is not from God." It was an act of Satan. Now, I rarely carried a handkerchief, but that night I reached into my pocket. I took a handkerchief, stood back up, and declared to the congregation, "I love you, but this is wrong." I wiped that handkerchief back and forth over my shoes as a symbolic display "wiping the dust from my shoes," like Jesus taught His disciples to do when people were not receptive to the gospel. It was a testimony against those wicked men. I took my wife, Charlotte, by the hand, and departed from the church, never to return as pastor. I was crushed. I hurt very deeply. I thought I was going to die from my terribly broken heart.

I wish I could say everything was perfect after that night. Miraculously, Charlotte and I continued to be blessed because I was attending seminary at the time, and my seminary professors, men of God, constantly prayed over me. Our chancellor would see me weeping in chapel and would stop the chapel service and pray over me. He understood what I had experienced. He was the one who had given me the advice to fire a disloyal associate pastor. It had to be done. The pain and the hurt grew worse and worse. The next Sunday we met with a few of the loyal folks who stood alongside us in the insurrection. As a result, a new church was born; needless to say, this move came with insurmountable struggles. At this point, I was faced with a housing dilemma. Charlotte and I had been living in the church parsonage and were forced to move into a small rental house. We decided we wanted to own our own home. Knowing our credit was good, we applied for a loan to purchase a modest, mobile home with plans to put it on the seminary campus. Much to our surprise, we were turned down for a loan! I had never been denied a loan. Even with great credit we were denied a loan. But God was working in my situation despite my hurt. Frankly, the purchase of a 12X60 "wobbly box" would have been a financial disaster. God was protecting me from myself. So, God directed me to apply for a home loan. We had a little bit of money in our savings and had purchased a lot in a beautiful upscale subdivision. Complete shock was our response when the phone call came informing us that our application for a home loan had been approved! Imagine that! We were unable to qualify for loan on a mobile home but were approved for a home loan. So, what did we do? *We built our dream house!* I barely earned any money at all while attending seminary and suffered from a condition I refer to as "mal- tuition". (Defined as the state of paying college/seminary tuition and being left totally broke!) I would go to seminary on Tuesdays and have a little money for tuition and say, "Take this. I'm going to class. Apply this to my bill. When this money runs out, come get me out of class, but I'm going to learn something while I am here!" They would laugh and send me to class.

It was a time of uncertainty, worse than I had ever experienced. We built a beautiful home; contracted it ourselves, and attended seminary, while attempting to pastor our small, newly formed church. Charlotte had a full-time job.

As our new home was nearing completion a vacant lot located four doors down from our house was on the market for sale. The lot sold. Strangely enough, the purchaser was the very man who led the insurrection six months earlier that resulted in my being fired. His plan was to build an investment home in *my* neighborhood, on *my* street, and *four doors down from my* house!

I asked, *"God, are You mad at me?"* After being fired from the church, I never expected to see that man again, and now, I was forced to see him almost every day. I still questioned, "God, are you tormenting me? It feels as though You're rubbing salt in this wound and You know I am hurting." Finally, after several months of this misery, the house was completed and was placed on the real estate market for sale. It remained unsold for months. Without a sale, the burden of the interim financing was devastating to the owner. There were rumors that he would lose the house. Within my heart, I wanted to think he had gotten what he deserved. I wanted to think that God was punishing him for the devastation and hurt he had caused me. But God's direction and grace overpowered my vengeful attitude. One day I stood at the kitchen sink inside our beautiful home. The Lord spoke to me and told me to pray - pray specifically for the house four doors down to sell. As I relayed this to Charlotte, I could hardly believe the words coming from my mouth! *Why was God telling me to pray for him? He was the man who had destroyed my first pastorate! He was the man who led all those people to make a foolish decision and have me fired!* I thought I was losing my mind. *Me - pray for him? This could not be happening!*

However, Charlotte and I began praying for God to bless that man. We prayed for God to send a buyer for his house. In the back of my mind I hoped if it didn't sell, surely, he wouldn't move into that house... and become my neighbor! However, that was not my motive for prayer. God was getting me into a position to where I had the heart to pray for someone who had caused me much devastating loss. Shortly afterwards the house sold, and my conscience was clear. My heart was right before God. Lesson learned! The man who caused me to be fired from my first pastoral position had been forgiven! I PASSED THE TEST! *Luke 6:28 NKJV, "Bless those who curse you and pray for those who spitefully use you." Matthew 5:44 NKJV, "But I say unto you, love your enemies, bless those who curse you, do good to those who hate you, and pray for those which spitefully use you, and persecute you."*

You may have a similar story. We have all suffered unjust and wrongdoing. All that matters now is that we are on the journey of healing, and we begin by taking the first step. We must be Christ- like and have a forgiving heart.

In the course of reading this book, some of you have played a DVD in the second track of your minds. You may think you don't want to relive the hurt.

You may feel that you cannot emotionally deal with the offenses. I want to give you some answers. The word *forgive* has a long definition. It takes several English words in order to expound on the Greek. When I began to study the Greek word forgive, this definition helped me to clearly understand its meaning: *Untie.* Visualize that you have restrained a wild horse. He kicks, he snorts, and he paws at the ground. He tries frantically to rear up and free himself. The rope is secure. The knot is secure. Then you decide of your own volition to set him free. You untie the rope and watch as the majestic animal is released into the wild. With his head held high and with strong determination, he gallops away until he is out of sight. Can you visualize that?

Now, here is the beauty of the spiritual power of forgiving. When we *untie* someone by forgiving him or her, we understand what we were unable to fathom before. That person, the offender, has lived rent-free in our minds. He mentally and emotionally intimidated us by kicking, snorting, and pawing. Possibly a smell or even a sound brings that person to your memory. The smallest trigger brings his face to your mind. You may hear a similar voice and the offense comes rushing back to torment you. However, to forgive means to untie the offender. When we untie him, we experience freedom that is indescribable and can only come from a loving God who wants us to enjoy an abundant life of peace, joy and love! When we set our offenders free, *we* are the ones who gain the truest form of freedom! When we untie them, we are the ones who are set free!

There are blessings that come when we obey God and forgive our offenders. Here is the rest of the story from earlier in this chapter. Not long after we forgave the person who built his investment house four doors down from our house, God directed us to relocate in another ministry. The housing market was still at an all-time low, but we listed our house with a realtor anyway. *Six weeks* from the day we listed our house, we went to closing. We were paid asking price for our house and had two back up offers! It was a miracle from God!

Power Questions and Action Points

1. Describe a time or circumstance when you ran out of options but continued to search for options. i.e. financial or family issues

2. What issues of your past have seen skeletons in your closet?

3. Of the eight forms of abuse listed in this chapter, which abuses have you experienced?

4. Stop and envision the word picture of untying your offender.

CHAPTER 2

Forgiving Is An Act Of The Will, Not An Act Of The Emotions

Forgiving people is an act of the will; not an act of our emotions. I believe it is life changing when you and I learn how to forgive the people who have hurt us. Forgiveness shines a light on the glory of God and removes any credit that may be directed to us. Let's review the "Model Prayer" that Jesus prayed. At the end of it, He gave us a command in Matthew 6: 14 NKJV,

14 "For if you forgive men their trespasses, your heavenly Father will also forgive you. 15 But if you do not forgive men their trespasses, neither will your Father forgive your trespasses."

Jesus taught us to remember that the word *if* means there is an option. We have a choice in every situation. We cannot choose *how* we get hurt or *who* hurts us; however, we can always choose *our response to the offense.* Jesus says if you forgive men their trespasses He will forgive your trespasses. The term *trespass* here is not the same word as *iniquity*, which is a lifestyle of sin. Nor is it the same word as *sin* found In Romans 3:23, "For all have sinned..." *Trespass* here means that someone has stepped over into your space. For instance, if you have a piece of land and you do not want anyone on it, you put up signs that say, *No Trespassing.* When someone has hurt you, they have stepped over into your life where clearly, they should not be. They have caused damage in an area of your life that was off limits.

So, let's address this next subject: What about situations where *we are the offender?* The bottom line is we have been guilty of hurting people! Often times, we have been the offender! We don't want to admit that. You may say, "Pastor, you should have put this as the last chapter in your book or I may throw the book down after a few chapters." Please read on. We must confront what we have done to people as well. There are times *we* need to be forgiven. Jesus says if you forgive people, God will forgive you.

Does God hear every prayer we pray? Certainly He does! God doesn't only hear everything we pray, He also knows everything we think. Is that a little frightening? I know it is for me. If you were to take a USB thumb drive and download everything that's going on my "ADHD brain" and view it on a computer, you would be shocked. Do not be judgmental of me; I'm sure the same can be said of your thought life as well! Our thought lives do not define who we are, they define the battlefields on which we are fighting. The point is God knows everything we think. He knows everything we say. God hears every prayer, but that does not mean God will honor or answer that prayer. It says in our text, if you have not forgiven others, God will not forgive you. I was enjoying the Model Prayer. I was enjoying the part about our giving God all the honor and glory that is due to Him, having His will be done on Earth and in Heaven, and praying for daily bread. Suddenly, Jesus changes the subject and addresses the sin of not forgiving those who have offended us which results in my not being forgiven! Whoa! Now look at the word *forgive*. I want you to underline this word in your Bible. The word *forgive* can seem somewhat vague. The Greek word is ἀφίημι (afiemi). Instead of using just one word, here is the broader meaning of the word. It is a separation or departure; completion; to send or send forth; to cry out; forsaking and laying aside; to leave or send away; to remit; to suffer in our forgiving; or to yield up. Having all these definitions of this one word is the beauty of the Greek language. Here again we use this definition: *to untie.*

I have given you the first principle; now I want to give you the second. We must discover how to forgive people so that the healing can begin. In review, the first principle was *forgiveness is not an option.* The next truth is this: *Forgiving other people is an act of the will, not an act of the emotions.* You and I must not be tempted to live our lives strictly by depending on our emotions. The emotional portion of the human brain does not possess the ability in which to discern facts or make logical decisions. Therefore, we cannot depend on our emotions when it comes to making decisions or discerning truth. We must make decisions based on facts and live in the truth of the Word of God. When it comes to forgiving people, we cannot allow our emotions to play a part in our decisions. Often times our emotions feel that the offender does not deserve forgiveness. After all, look what he did to me! Allow me to share a *lesson from the hayfield.*

My dad, Delos Husser, was a missionary pastor. He was instrumental in starting a church in Slidell, Louisiana. The church had a rocky beginning but eventually began to thrive. It wasn't long before that little church was packed full of folks every Sunday. One night when my dad and a deacon were visiting in the community, they realized that one of the ladies in our church hadn't attended in a few Sundays, so they dropped by her house to check on her. Now back then, there were no cell phones and most people didn't even have home phones! Of course, a phone call was not made before you visited in someone's home; you simply dropped by their house. My dad and that faithful deacon approached the little trailer park where the lady lived. There were several cars in her driveway. They knocked on the door, and much to their surprise, the little mobile home was packed with people who were members of my dad's church. When my dad and the deacon walked inside, those people had the look of "a deer caught in headlights!" They were like a crawfish looking at a Cajun! They did not know if they should run backwards or simply jump into the boiling pot! They were as surprised to see my dad as he was surprised to see them! Come to find out, they were having a meeting to organize an insurrection to take over the church and fire my dad as pastor. Also, the lady who owned this home had formerly been involved in witchcraft, which is prevalent in South Louisiana. This should have been an indication of her character. As a result of these few people, led by one ungodly woman, the church imploded within a month or so later. Many people followed her and left the church. I was only a young boy, but I remember this tragedy as though it were yesterday. My dad was hurt very deeply because he loved that church and had devoted many years of his life to its growth.

Now, let's fast-forward to the year 1976. Our family now lived in Franklinton, Louisiana, where my dad owned land and raised beef cattle. One day my telephone rang. It was "that woman". The very same woman who had been guilty of destroying our church in Slidell back 1969. We had not seen her or had any contact with her for more than seven years. When she identified herself, I immediately felt I should hang up the phone; but I didn't. She asked to speak to my dad, who was in the hayfield at the time. She said, "Louis,

I'm looking for your daddy. Last night my son was involved in a car accident and was killed." She continued, "I need your daddy to officiate his funeral." I could not believe what I was hearing! How could a woman who had been extremely vindictive to my dad have the nerve to ask such a thing from him? I hung up the phone and drove out into the hayfield. On the drive, I thought to myself, "This is going to be a joke. Why does she need my dad after all she did to hurt him so deeply and to cause so much harm and division in the Lord's church?"

When I reached his location in the field, he was busy gathering and bailing hay. Most of the time his old hay equipment malfunctioned and this time was no different. I said to my dad, "You're never going to believe who just called!" He asked, "Who?" I told him her name and he said, "Okay, what does she want?" I related the details of her phone call to him, and said, "Dad, you are not going to believe this. Of all people, she wants *you* to officiate the service for her son's funeral!" Now I thought he was going to give me the difficult task of calling her back and declining her request. Actually, that's *exactly* what my response would have been. However, my dad immediately stopped what he was doing and told his workers he would call them back to finish in a couple of days. He was going to help a family in need. He did not hesitate. He did not consider all the devastation that woman had previously inflicted on his life. He did not consider his own feelings. He knew that God had given him another opportunity to minister to a family who had never known the forgiving grace of Jesus Christ. He knew he needed to be obedient to His calling of the ministry and to crucify his emotions. He did just that.

My dad taught me more about the importance of forgiving people in that old hayfield that day than I learned in four years of seminary. I also learned another very important reality from that experience. Here is it: JUST BECAUSE WE DO WHAT IS RIGHT, DOESN'T MEAN WE ARE GOING TO FEEL RIGHT. Just do the right thing anyway. The urgency of sharing the good news of the gospel superseded my dad's emotions.

This statement bears repeating: Forgiveness is not an act of the emotions, it is an act of the will. Always do the "right thing".

In Galatians 2:20 NKJV, Paul was able to forgive people. Writing to the church in Galatia, he said, *20 "I have been crucified with Christ; it is no longer I who live, but Christ lives in me; and the life which I now live in the flesh I live by faith in the Son of God, who loved me and gave Himself for me."*

Now you may ask, "What does that have to do with forgiveness?" You and I will never *feel* like forgiving our offenders because of how severely we have been hurt. They've altered our lives. Some of you have had your childhood stolen from you because of sexual abuse, and yet you continue to refuse to forgive that person. You and I must learn to take our unforgiving emotions, which are not in line with the Word of God and nail them to the cross. Harboring angry feelings is not justified. Those feelings must be crucified and covered in the blood of Christ; otherwise they will ruin us emotionally.

I Thessalonians 5:23 NKJV, "Now may the God of peace Himself sanctify you completely;" which means obviously, the process of sanctification is, in fact, just that. It's a process. God is the only way to real peace and in this process, forgiving is one of the steps. You and I cannot fabricate peace. It is God's peace; it is not our peace. If you say you can't find peace, it's because you haven't found God; but when you find God, His peace is made available to you!

"And may your whole spirit, soul, and body be preserved blameless at the coming of our Lord us Christ". Let's closely consider these 3 words: *body, soul,* and *spirit.*

I want to help you to understand yourself. You have a *body*. It's your body; your flesh and bones, muscle, tissue, blood, organs, etc. *Spirit* is the part of you that never dies. When you became born again, Jesus moved into and now dwells within your spirit. This next word is where the entire moderate, cultural, and nominal Christian runs into a train wreck. You have a *soul.* The word soul is the word ψυχή (psuchē) in the Greek; our word *psychology* comes from this word. We have a body, we have a spirit, and we have this thing called a soul. The soul is the housing compartment of our mind, will, and emotions. When a person dies, those three die as well; but until then, we have a battle raging. The battle is in our minds, wills, and emotions.

Romans 12: 1-2 NKJV, "I beseech you therefore, brethren, by the mercies of God, that ye present your bodies a living sacrifice, holy, acceptable to God, which is your reasonable service. 2. And do not conformed to this world, but be

TRANSFORMED BY THE RENEWING OF YOUR MIND that ye may prove what is that good and acceptable, and perfect will of God."

That is why the Bible tells us to be "transformed by the renewing of our minds." I need the mind of Jesus because I don't approve of the way my mind thinks. Many times, my carnal thinking hinders the work of Christ in me. This is the reason a quiet time with the Lord is vital. We should spend time in His Word *DAILY!*

Philippians 2: 5-8 NKJV, "Let this mind be in you which was in Christ Jesus. 6. Who being in the form of God, did not consider it robbery to be equal with God. 7. But made himself of no reputation, taking the form of a bondservant, and coming in the likeness of men. 8. And being found in appearance as a man, He humbled Himself, and became obedient to the point of death, even the death of the cross."

I don't approve of the "thought life" of Louis Husser; therefore, I must die to myself in order to have the mind of Christ. I want Him to take charge and control my emotions. Now allow me to clarify that statement. For those of you who are "emos", emotions are not all bad. Jesus Christ was *all* God and *all* man, not half God and half man. So, during His earthly ministry, He had emotions. When Jesus saw the multitude of people dying and going to hell without faith in Him, this caused Him to weep for their sinful condition. He cried out to God. He says in *Matthew 23:37 NKJV, "Oh, Jerusalem, Jerusalem, the one who kills the prophets and stones those who are sent to her! How often I wanted to gather your children together, as a hen gathers her chicks under her wings, but ye were not willing!*

Christ expressed His emotions as He observed the lost! By the way, if you want to be emotional about something, be emotional about your neighbors not having Christ in their lives. Feel the emotion of compassion that Jesus Christ experienced. Even as He was about to raise Lazarus from the dead, the Bible says, "Jesus wept". This is the shortest verse in all the Bible, but it speaks volumes. *John 11:35 – 36 NKJV, "JESUS WEPT. Then said the Jews said, ' See how He loved him!'"* The middle of those two words speaks volumes about how Jesus expressed His emotions. He was familiar with the emotion of sorrow. When our emotions do not line up with the truth of the Word of God, they must be crucified. God does not want our emotions to be that of a doormat or of *victim mentality*. Neither does He want ours to be that of a wallflower with no personality at all. Jesus had emotions as a human and He expressed them.

There is need for caution about our emotions. As a Christian you cannot allow yourself to slip into the philosophy of "It is all about how you feel". You must learn who you are "in Christ". You must have a relationship with Christ and know how to identify false emotions by developing the art of having the mind of Christ. If you have a relationship with the Holy Spirit, and your emotions rise up and tell you to hate a person for what they did, you must pause and allow the Holy Spirit to convict you of that sin and quickly repent and turn from it. But what if you say you have no emotions at all? When Christ tells us to crucify the flesh, He didn't intend for us to be emotionless. When we die to ourselves, He will resurrect us. I'm here to say that no one can pull off a resurrection like God the Father. He can make it happen. We need to learn that when we die to our emotions, it is not as though we remain dead to ourselves. It means that *we die* to our own desires, that Christ comes into our lives and gives us real life and emotions that line up with the Scriptures. That's what God wants for His children. He wants us to be complete and whole in Him.

Now, I want to challenge you. Study your Bible every day of your life. You need to spend time finding out what God says about the hurt you have experienced as well as to help you to grow in your faith.

Allow me to recap. The second reality is this: *Forgiving other people is an act of the will, not an act of the emotions.*

I am not into the philosophy of "Name It and Claim It". I don't buy into the bad theology of you "speak it into existence." It never worked when at the age of thirty. I began to lose my hair. I would stand in front of a mirror and say, "I am claiming hair. I'm claiming it!" As you can clearly see, it did not work. You can't stand in front of a bank and claim to be a millionaire. You will remain broke. That is bad theology because it is selfishly based.

However, the Bible does say in *Proverbs 18:21 NKJV, "Death and life are in the power of the tongue, and those who love it will eat its fruit."* So, there is a need to examine that Scripture within context. Forgiving people is not an

FORGIVING Others

evolutionary process. It is a point in time decision. This scripture refers to two different events: one is death and the other is life. Remember this. Death is a point in time; life is a point in time. I am not going to *gradually* hope that I get to a point of feeling better about forgiving a person. I must forgive at an intentional, *point in time. I choose to forgive.* I forgive. These are two of the most powerful words in the English language.

There is something intriguing about the mind and glory of God. When God chose to create man and woman, He wanted them to have a choice called *free will.* God did not make a mistake by giving us some level of choosing and choices, because look how Adam blew it when he sinned in the Garden of Eden. You give a guy a choice and what does he do? He blows it. Right? Now, don't get mad at Adam. If Adam hadn't been the one who first sinned, it would've been somebody else - most likely ME! If not me, it could have been YOU! Thankfully, God has instilled in every one of us the *will to choose.* I'm not a fatalist. The Bible doesn't teach the philosophy of "whatever will be – will be." You and I still have a choice in the matter. God is not going to force a salvation experience onto you by violating your free will. However, God does leave some decisions up to us. We do not choose our own destiny. Some things happened to us by the will of others.

We live in the south not far from the Gulf of Mexico. Hurricanes are the norm for us. Now, we do not get to choose what a hurricane does to us, but we do get to decide to evacuate or not. By the same token, you and I have been given the freedom to choose to forgive those who have hurt us. We cannot choose the direction of the wind. However, we can choose how we set our sail. We must choose wisely.

Now let's look at *MATTHEW 21: 21 NJKV, "So Jesus answered and said to them, "Assuredly, I say to you, if you have faith and do not doubt, you will not only do what was done to the fig tree, but also if you say to this mountain, 'Be removed and be cast into the sea,' it will be done."* When I committed my life to the Lord in December of 1973, I began reading my Bible every day. I started with the Gospels. I was amazed when I came to this verse and Jesus spoke about moving mountains! I read those Scriptures and thought, "Well, moving mountains…" First off, do you and I have the power to physically speak to a mountain and relocate it? When I think of moving mountains, visualization is somewhat difficult. In my area of the country, South Louisiana has no mountains, and very few hills. I would sit at my kitchen table and see nothing but flat land. Maybe that is not what God was talking about. *Do we need a physical mountain to be moved?* If we do, God has blessed someone with the ability to create hydraulics, put it on a Caterpillar dozer, and there we go! We can move that mountain! So, what exactly is Jesus referring to in this Scripture? Here is one application I would like to share with you. When I fail to forgive people, a mountain of bitterness can arise. It is a mountain so high I can't get over it, around it, or under it. I can't dig through it. So here is this mountain of unforgiveness that Jesus says to cast into the sea! That's powerful!

You may think I am misapplying this text. The biggest mountain I have is forgiving people who have hurt me. You can seek forgiveness, and God says He can move that mountain of bitterness out of your life!

Christ wants us to make wise choices. He wants us to make a conscience decision to forgive those who have offended us. We do this as an act of the *will*.

In our Western culture, we communicate through our feelings. We express ourselves by using our feelings. For example, we may say, "Well, I feel like...", or "Well, let me tell you how I feel about it." If we have a life filled with pain, too often things that come out of our mouths are just an expression of the hurt on the inside. God says there is a better way to communicate. The Hebrews of the Bible, especially the prophets, would communicate a message, not in feelings and emotions, but communicate in word pictures or stories referred to as parables. Isn't that amazing? Those prophets and writers could paint a type of a word picture that feelings and emotions could never express. It is as though it were on a theatrical stage and you could visualize the story as it unfolds. A visual illustration is much better than expressing a story based on how we "feel" about the subject.

Perhaps, we would be better off to use a physical illustration. Now why am I saying all this? Because when Jesus referred to untying and forgiving people, He painted a word picture. Jesus Christ was obviously the master teacher, the master communicator, the master of setting up a theatrical scene, so that you and I can say, " I've got the picture. I understand it." It's one thing to hear; it's another thing to *see what you are hearing.* Did you comprehend what I just said? People sit in church every Sunday and hear the Word repeatedly, but seem to miss the message. So, if we see it as it unfolds, we gain a clear communication of the message. Again, let me use this illustration. When Jesus taught on *untying*, he painted a word picture of an animal standing tied. As it stands there for a long period of time, our compassion compels us to take action and untie the animal. We deliberately take action to untie the rope and set the captive free. Here is the word picture that those Hebrew people would have understood. We move toward and untie that animal. Now here is the mystery of that one message. When you and I choose to forgive people, we become untied! We are the ones who obtain freedom! The strange thing about our minds is when someone has hurt us, and we refuse to forgive them, we are the one who are tied up. We are the ones who are bound and limited, because the person who has hurt us so deeply lives rent-free in our minds. In a split-second, you and I can replay the entire incident. Why not set yourself free?

Here in south Louisiana we have two references of time: *before* Hurricane Katrina and *after* Hurricane Katrina that devastated large portions of

Louisiana and the Mississippi Gulf coast in 2005. Not many months after Hurricane Katrina hit the Gulf Coast, some missionary friends of ours from the Dominican Republic came to visit for a few days. They wanted to ride horses. At that time, my daughter and I were in competitive barrel racing, so we saddled up and rode on our farm. Finally, after a while, I said. "Let me show y'all what we do to have fun." I had three barrels set up in our pasture. I rode one of our better barrel horses and zipped through the first two barrels, and at the third barrel, the horse stiffened his neck, so I kicked him twice. When I did, within a split-second, we were both on the ground with him lying on my right leg. I instantly realized my leg was in a great deal of pain. I did what every other good husband would do. I yelled, "CHARLOTTE! Please come!" (Billy Graham made Franklin Graham, his son, promise that when he died, Franklin would take him back to Charlotte, North Carolina. When I heard that, I was like, *Yep, when I die someone take me to Charlotte.* For those of you reading, it's a play on words because my wife's name is Charlotte.) It has now been thirteen years later. Every morning when I get out of bed, I hear that snap, crackle, and pop. You have just seen a word picture that explains how easily it is for the least insignificant detail to remind us of past hurts. Every morning I am reminded about that horse falling on my leg.

The wife of that missionary couple was in medical school in the Dominican Republic. We wanted to take her to an American hospital, so that she could tour the hospital. Up until this point, our busy schedule had not allowed a tour. Suddenly, we are at the hospital, and she was privileged to tour the hospital with the granddaughter of the great Dr. Alton Ochsner, Sr., the founder of Ochsner Health Center.

Power Questions and Action Points

1. List goals that you accomplished as a result of your persistent will.

2. How have your emotions lead you into wrong decisions in your past?

3. List at least 5 emotional decisions that have had bad outcomes. How often do you begin a statement with "I feel, I felt, or I felt like…?"

4. List the inspiring people in your life who have exemplified a forgiving attitude.

5. What experiences of your past have you done the "right thing" but did not feel good as a result of your actions?

6. What false emotions are you struggling with that need to be crucified?

CHAPTER 3

It's Not Within Us to Forgive

Everything affects us. Every event in our lives, whether good or bad, results in the formation of our emotional makeup. There are times when we must unpack life's negative events to make sense of our emotions. Healing cannot take place until we do this. Whether there is an abandoned parent, or any type of abuse, the hurt runs very deeply and can significantly alter our lives. Because of that, we can go directly to the Word of God to find the answers.

We've all been guilty of saying that you simply need to forgive people who have offended you. I have been guilty of making that statement in the past. Many well- meaning Christians say, "You simply need to forgive that person." The bottom line is the lack of knowledge of how to properly forgive only leads to more frustration for the individual who has been offended. We must be taught Biblical forgiveness. Without forgiveness, healing cannot take place. It is impossible. The hurt is still present and as a matter of fact, over time, it can become significantly worse resulting in broken relationships. A person with a wounded spirit has difficulty with trust in other people.

Another bit of bad advice is, being told to "simply get over it". This also presents more frustration and compounds the problem. A change in our emotions must come as a result in action taken on our part. To simply "get over it" will not alter our emotions or enable us to forgive.

More bad advice is to "Forgive and forget". If we do not know how to forgive, we certainly do not have the capacity to forget! The truth is that deep hurts are never simply forgotten. They are deeply imbedded in our minds; sometime consciously and sometimes subconsciously. They remain as long as our memory serves us. So, how do we handle this dilemma? We must to go to the Word of God for answers. When people are deeply hurt, many times the blame for the offense is misplaced. Victims may try to justify their offender by saying, "Oh, he really did not mean what he said", or "That's just his personality." Actually, we are all responsible for every word that comes from our mouths. *Romans 14:12 NKJV "So then each of us shall give an account of himself to God."* With the understanding that we are personally responsible, we cannot justify our offender's actions. He must be confronted.

There is a valid reason for us to remember our offenses. As long as we have the memory of an offense, we may be in a position to prevent it from happening again. God does not intend for us to be a "doormat" or in a constant state of being the victim! He intends for us to break free from the chains of an offender. If we ignore an offense, this places us back under the authority and power of the offender. No one benefits from "ignoring", especially if the offender is not aware of the offense. Our hearts must be open and honest before God. Now, on the other hand, God does not remember our offenses against us, once we have been forgiven. *Micah 7:19 NKJV, "He will turn again, He will have compassion upon us. He will subdue our iniquities. You will cast all our sin into the depths of the sea."* Only God can "forgive and forget!"

Another form of misplaced blame is when individuals blame God for their hurts. It is very easy to think that God could have prevented the tragedy; therefore, it is *His* fault we feel this way. Blaming God is NEVER a good idea! The truth is, God has created humans with a "free will". We all have a sinful or carnal nature. God is not responsible for the horrible events of our lives, but He is there to lovingly pick us up and heal our wounds. This cannot happen if we blame Him for the actions committed by evil people. The result of blaming God is an unjustified anger toward Him and a total misunderstanding of *who He really is.*

I have known many people who are angry at God. You say, "Yeah, that's really strange. Why would someone want to come to church if they are angry at God?" You may be surprised of all that has happened to cause their anger. Can you imagine that? A person must have a lot of backbone in order to be angry with God! He can snuff us out very quickly!

One of my favorite movies is *God's Not Dead.* Kevin Sorbo plays the part of an atheist professor who gave a student much grief because he was a believer in Christ. Finally, the young, Godly student asked Kevin Sorbo a sobering question. He asked, "What happened to you for you to be bitter toward God?" I believe we should ask ourselves that question. Have we constructed any walls of bitterness or anger in our lives that would prevent God's love from penetrating our hearts? The key is one of the greatest answers I have ever found in the Word of God and will help in the quest of forgiving people. The answer is not emotional; it is *spiritual*. Let's explore Jesus' teachings in Luke 23. The death, burial and resurrection are recorded in all four gospels, but we'll choose Luke. Let's begin with verse 32. *"There were also two others, criminals, led with Him to be put to death. 33 And when they had come to the place called Calvary, there they crucified Him, and the criminals, one on the right hand and the other on the left. 34 Then Jesus said, "Father, forgive them, for they do not know what they do." And they divided His garments and cast lots. 35 And the people stood looking on. But even the rulers with them sneered, saying, "He saved others; let Him save Himself if He is the Christ, the chosen of God." 36 The soldiers also mocked Him, coming and offering Him sour wine, 37 and saying, "If You are the King of the Jews, save Yourself." 38 And an inscription also was written over Him in letters of Greek, Latin, and Hebrew: THIS IS THE KING OF THE JEWS."*

Luke 24: 1-2 NKJV, 1 "Now on the first day of the week, very early in the morning, they, and certain other women with them, came to the tomb bringing the spices which they had prepared. 2 But they found the stone rolled away from the tomb. 3 Then they went in and did not find the body of the Lord Jesus".

Let's go back to Luke 23. As Christ hung on the cross, shedding His precious life's blood for our sins, He made seven statements, one of which He asks His Father to forgive those who placed Him there. He was put there unjustly. It was an unfair execution. If every one of us wrote down every sin we committed throughout our entire lifetime, the result of these would never compare to the insurmountable suffering Christ felt on the cross.

When I was a child, my grandmother had pictures in her house of Christ hanging on the cross. Of course, the picture mildly portrayed His atrocious suffering. My dad, as a preacher, would always say, "Son, those are good pictures, but I want you to understand something. In every picture that humans could possibly paint of the brutal suffering of the Lord Jesus Christ, there is no comparison to the actual physical, emotional, and spiritual agony He experienced." In Christ's perfection, He experienced the sin of all of mankind. That cannot be portrayed in a picture, nor can millions of words come close to explaining His suffering. Unfortunately, my dad didn't live long enough to see the movie, Mel Gibson's *The Passion of The Christ*. In my opinion, the movie is the best possible portrayal of the events of Christ's sufferings. I think if my dad had seen that movie, he would have still had the same opinion. I must agree!

We are humanly deficient when it comes to comprehending His love for us as He suffered on the cross. Therefore, whatever you and I have suffered as hurts and offenses, it holds no light to how our Lord Jesus Christ was offended, heart- broken, and mistreated. You may say, "But you don't understand what I have been through." No, I may not, but one thing is for sure. You can spend your life obsessing over that hurt, but unless you dwell on THE ANSWER, you will spend the remainder of your life as a miserable person. So, what do we do? Let's examine one of the seven sayings of the cross: *Luke 23: 34 NKJV,* *"FATHER, FORGIVE THEM FOR THEY DO NOT KNOW WHAT THEY DO."* First of all, what an insult to Christ to hang him between two criminals! The very Son of God, reduced to the level of death at the hands of Roman soldiers, but more so humiliating to die between thieves! His overwhelming compassion allowed Him to ask for forgiveness of his murderers! "FATHER, FORGIVE THEM". This is one of the seven statements He made as He was dying on the cross, and I believe it is the most powerful! What great and indescribable love Christ has for us!

Now, you and I have a command from the Word of God to forgive people. There is a direct correlation between the act of forgiving and of our worship, giving, and our faith. Unforgiveness affects every area of our lives, physically, emotionally, and spiritually. So, somebody comes along who has a little bit of spirituality and says, "Well, you simply need to forgive all those people who have hurt you." You say, "I can't." You are correct. It is not within our abilities as humans to forgive the people who have hurt or offended us. There's a powerful answer in that fact. Give up on it and don't even try it. You know why? It's because the best of us are humanly flawed.

The best forgiveness that you and I could fabricate is still humanly flawed. It is so flawed that when we say that we forgive, if we do it within ourselves, guess what is going to happen. It is going to be flawed forgiveness. It is going to be the kind of forgiveness that if you hurt me again, I'm going to bring it up again. You've heard the old expression of "let's bury the hatchet"? The problem so often is that when we bury the hatchet, as humans, and we will leave the handle exposed so that when we are offended again we can conveniently grab the handle and defend ourselves with the hatchet of their past offense. It doesn't work. You say, "I'm feeling some relief already because I have been trying to forgive this person and I just can't get any relief." Well, surely you can't because any forgiveness that you and I can offer is flawed, broken and incomplete. So, what's the answer?

When Christ hung on the cross unjustly, He said, "*Father, forgive them for they do not know what they do.*" This is the kind of forgiveness we should have toward those who have offended us. When Christ said, "*Father, forgive them*", it was perfect and complete forgiveness. You say, "Yeah, but He was

Jesus." Well, I am glad you said that. Allow me to give to you the essence of Christianity. Allow Christ to live His life through you! *"To them God willed to make known what are the riches of the glory of this mystery among the Gentiles; which is Christ in you, the hope of glory." Colossians 1:27 NKJV*

It would be emotionally draining to attempt to figure out how to be a Christian or to fabricate all that we are supposed to do as believers. A lost person may sit in church and assume he could never be one of "those guys". His assumption is correct. He may think, "I can never quit all the bad habits I have. I can never forgive those who have harmed me." Many people fail at Christianity and blame God because they attempt to be a Christian in the energy of their own flesh, rather than with the aid of this one truth. *Christ showed perfect forgiveness on the cross.* As a believer in Him, I have placed my faith in Him. Each day I must allow His forgiveness to flow through me to the person I must forgive. It is Christ's forgiveness; not my forgiveness. Once you understand this, healing will become evident in your life. Every aspect of the Christian life is for Him, Jesus Christ, to live every day through us. *II Corinthians 2:10 NKJV, "Now whom you forgive anything, I also forgive. for if indeed I have forgiven anything, I have forgiven that one for your sakes in the presence of Christ."*

John 15: *4 NKJV, "Abide in Me, and I in you. As the branch cannot bear fruit of itself".* We cannot live the Christian life within ourselves. We can't forgive people. This information is valuable for those of you with teenagers. Often times, parents have trouble being patient with teen children. There is good news. You don't have to be patient with them; just allow the patience of Jesus Christ flow through you to your teenager. You may want to place them in lockdown for at least ten years! Jesus says, *4 "As the branch cannot bear fruit of itself, unless it abides in the vine, neither can you, unless you abide in Me."* It is His life flowing through us. Pause, and allow God to create a picture of this within your spiritual mind. This picture is very powerful. Now, what does it show? Every characteristic of Jesus MUST flow through us on a day to day basis. *What flows to us must flow through us.* Whatever we need, Christ is the supply. If we need love for people, or forgiveness toward people, we must allow Christ's provision to flow through us as an individual. *Galatians 5: 22-23 NKJV, "But the fruit of the Spirit is love, joy, peace, longsuffering, kindness, goodness, faithfulness, gentleness, self-control, against such there is no law."* That is true Christianity. You and I don't have to create the forgiveness for any horrible offense. The very perfect, complete forgiveness of Jesus Christ flows through us to that person. You ask, "Please give me something a little more foundational. Exactly what can I do?" I have learned that my mind will not let go. I remember the offense. You do as well. "But if I truly forgive this person, I should be able to forget it." No, no, no! Remember the "hatchet" illustration?

Here is the picture. Every time my mind replays the hurt, the offense, it is still here in my frontal lobe. How many of you play the "video" over and over again? A word or phrase, a smell, the smallest thing, etc. can trigger an instant recall. It is still very prevalent in our memories. But here is the power of the message of the cross. Every time my mind goes back into that deep hurt, I must discipline my spiritual mind, to see Jesus Christ, hanging on the cross, and I must rebuke that offense. Pray as Jesus Himself prayed, "Father, forgive them for they know not what they do." When I am reminded and that memory surfaces, I suddenly become tense. My pancreas begins to generate too much adrenaline. You know that sick feeling. You say, "Ugggggggghh, I just saw that person in the grocery store the other day. I just can't believe that God hasn't already struck him with a bolt of lightning. God, if you would ever let *me* be God, I'll get 'em!" When that memory begins to well up inside, you must quickly discipline your mind to see the message of the cross and see Jesus Christ as He asked His Father to forgive them! You must superimpose the mental picture of Christ on the cross and visualize His dying for that particular offense! He paid the penalty for that very sin. You can name the hurt you've suffered and put it right there on the cross.

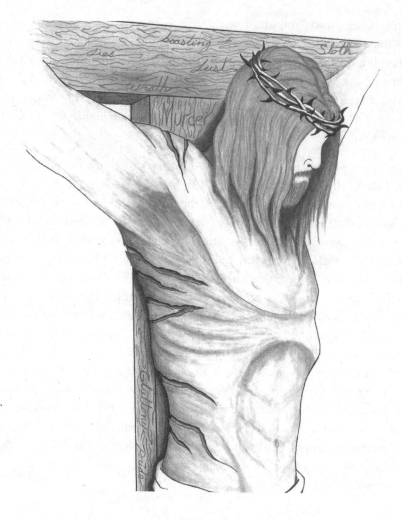

You see, the message of the cross is the only avenue there is for people to come into a relationship with Jesus Christ. We share the good news of the cross; of the death, burial, and resurrection of Jesus Christ, and people repent of their sin. The Bible refers to this transformation as being born again. So often we share the gospel with folks, they come to Christ, and think, "Okay, this is good. Now, I want to learn all those fun things about how to gain prosperity and health. Now that I'm a Jesus freak, I need to learn how to overcome anger at my spouse and so on." Christianity is not a behavioral modification program. It doesn't work that way. You see, we bring people to Christ and explain the message of His sacrifice on the cross. As believers we must teach new Christians to live for Christ on a daily basis. We should remember His sacrifice and live each day with His holy life as our example. The message of the cross is not a traffic stop along the road of life. We should *stay* at the cross.

So, what is the message of the cross? How do I do that? The more we envision Christ on the cross, dying for the offense that hurt us so deeply, that offense begins to move from frontal lobe to the back of our brains. The picture of the hurt will no longer occupy our dominant thoughts. The video gets stored in the back closet of our minds and does not surface until it needs to be used to help others. I don't know about you, but the more I envision the offense, I want to say, "Jesus, I can't forgive that person. But God, You said that You forgave them and I'm allowing Your forgiveness to flow through me to that person." I allow you to give me a change of heart.

Years ago, my wife and I traveled nationwide in professional Christian music and evangelism, singing and preaching in many great churches. We traveled in a customized motor coach. To illustrate this kind of forgiveness, New Mexico comes to mind, where the low lands begin. I remember many nights as we finished a concert, revival meeting or crusade, we would leave from a church parking lot and drive west toward California. We would get a few miles out of town where I could look in the rearview mirror and could see the entire city inside that rearview mirror. We would continue driving west, going up the ascent. It was as if the lights would get smaller as we continued driving. Instead of taking up the entire rearview mirror, the city lights would appear smaller in the mirror. Every few miles I could look back and as we drove farther away, the city was nothing more than a speck in the rearview mirror. It would appear barely visible. We should learn from this illustration that the key is to continue moving toward new heights in the Lord! The more I envision what Christ did on the cross to forgive those people who have hurt me, the further I keep moving forward and seeing Christ on the cross. That's why the Scripture refers to Jesus as "The Author and Finisher of our faith." Hebrews 12:2 NKJV, *"Looking unto Jesus the Author and Finisher of our faith; who for the joy that was set before Him endured the cross, despising the shame, and has sat down at the right hand of the throne of God."* Time does not heal any wounds. Time alone does nothing but drive the pain deeper. God uses time for *us* to be healed.

If you keep your eyes on people, you will continue to be hurt. They will cause you to be disillusioned. People do not always present a true picture of Christianity. Only Christ can do this. "Well, I'm not going to church because there are so many hypocrites there." If you are looking for hypocrites at church, you're going to find them. In response to that statement, I told a guy the other day, "Man, that's true. There are hypocrites in our church but come on anyway. One more isn't going hurt us! We've got room for one more!" Wherever you are looking, that's where you're going, and if you will keep looking toward Jesus Christ, you'll never see all this clutter around you. You keep looking to Jesus Christ because it is Him and Him alone who has given us His perfect forgiveness.

The healing will begin to take place when you realize that you don't have to forgive these people. Christ has forgiven them. He made His forgiveness available and I must allow everything He is to flow through me. That's the essence of Christianity. Look at 2 Corinthians 2:10 KJV. The apostle Paul is writing to a church that is so corrupt you would not join, but by the time the second letter arrived, the Word of God had corrected the church problems. *10 "To whom you forgive anything, I forgive also."* Now here is a guy who "took it on the chin" for his faith in Christ. He was offended and mistreated numerous times while ministering in the name of Jesus. *"For if indeed I have forgiven anything, I have forgiven that one for your sakes in the* person of Christ.*"*

The King James translation refers to this as *the person of Christ.* Now, let's stop and glean something out of that word. This is the best way to study our Bibles. He said, "If I forgave anyone", and I do believe that Paul had a long list of names of people to forgive. Look closely and you will see that Paul called them by name. You would never want to be on Paul's list of offenders! He confirms everything I have been teaching. The only way to forgive people is in the person or presence of Jesus Christ. Isn't that amazing? Isn't that a relief? I can take a deep breath now and realize, that my method of forgiving was not getting the desired results. I thought that I had to forgive those people, and the truth is that I must allow, be available, commit and surrender myself to allow Jesus Christ to live His life through me. It is not about *What Would Jesus Do? It's What Did Jesus Do*? He forgave them!

Thank God this struggle is over. I see the person who offended me and realize that he no longer has the authority to upset me. I visualize Jesus hanging on the cross saying, "Father, forgive them for they know not what they do." I tried to do this all on my own until I learned this truth. Now for thirty years I have been teaching these principles to people who come into my counseling office. They tell me their stories and I weep with them. I say to them, "Let me teach you something." As a matter of fact, I'll show you how, *what flows to us must flow through us*. Galatians 5:*22 NKJV, "But the fruit of the Spirit…"*

Only ONE fruit of the Holy Spirit, moved inside us at the moment of our spiritual birth. When you receive the Holy Spirit, you didn't get to pick and choose which one of these you're going to develop. You already have the fruit of the Spirit in you. You simply allow these Godly characteristics to be exemplified in your life.

While questioning Jesus on forgiveness, Peter asked how many times he should forgive somebody in a day? Seven times? Jesus' answer was seven times seventy in a twenty-four hour time span. It's going to take His love flowing through you to forgive that person. Within your own capabilities, you don't possess that type of love. It is not in us to unconditionally love people. It is not in us as humans. We are flawed, depraved. So, what is the "fruit of the Spirit"?

"Love" We are not capable of loving people with the unconditional love of Christ.

"Joy" It's not our joy. It's His joy in us.

"Peace" It's the peace of God within us.

"Longsuffering "Are you thinking of a name and face right now? Yep, it takes longsuffering to tolerate this person, and you can't do that on your own.

"Kindness" You can't be kind to that person.

"Goodness" You cannot return goodness for evil because it is not within us to do so. The best of us could never fabricate this; you can't fake it that long.

"Faithfulness" Can we be steadfast, unmovable, see a project through to the end?

"Gentleness" Not harsh or severe in our tone of voice.

"Self-control" Well, let's talk about self-control. What about the amount of food we eat? What about angry words that come from our months? This list could go on indefinitely!

These are all one single fruit. You say, "I'm going to be faithful, but I don't know about that longsuffering thing." You don't get to choose just one of these. When you get the Holy Spirit, you get them all and they become part of who you are. Isn't that an amazing truth? Here is the essence of it. Christ and the message of the cross is so powerful, that we should live at the cross every day. I want to show you a Scripture. *Galatians 2:20 NKJV, "I have been crucified with Christ; it is no longer I who live, but Christ lives in me and the life which I now live in the flesh I live by the faith in the Son of God who loved me and gave himself for me."* Only when we choose to die to ourselves...i.e., anger, bitterness, unforgiveness, etc. will God resurrect a new life within us. It will be a new life of peace, patience joy, etc. It took four days before Lazarus was resurrected from the dead. Jonah spent three days and nights in the belly of the big fish. Young Isaac followed his father, Abraham to a place of sacrifice while in his mind, Isaac was as good as dead for the journey of three days. Moses spent forty years waiting on God to resurrect him to usefulness as a leader. How long are you willing to remain "dead"? It is during the time of "waiting on God" as He is preparing you for your resurrection. Allow God to resurrect you!

If you can get your spiritual heart and mind *wrapped* around this passage in Galatians 2:20, you could live out the very thing you have been telling yourself that you cannot do. "I can't be one of those Christians." You're right... you can't. Jesus does not want fans; He wants followers. I am somewhat of a New Orleans Saints fan. Actually, I am a fair -weather fan; a fan only when they are winning. I don't want to be a *fan* of Jesus Christ, I want to be one of His *followers!* The apostle Paul said, "I have been crucified with Christ." Now that is a difficult way to sell books and videos and fill up mega-churches. If we preach this in conjunction with Jesus saying, "If anyone wants to follow after Me, let him deny himself, take up his cross, and follow Me." Our church congregations would be much smaller. Christianity is not about your convenience. Jesus said if anyone will follow after Me, let him deny himself and take up his cross. If I have truly been crucified with Christ, my life will not revolve around my wants and wishes. Life is not about me. Even in the secular world, companies hire motivational speakers to speak to their employees. They pay exuberant amounts of money. That is all fine. Even they will teach you, in order to be successful in life, you cannot focus on yourself. You must focus on others! Imagine that.

Allow me to paraphrase Paul's words, "I've been crucified with Christ. It is no longer I who lives, but Christ who lives through me." His forgiveness is alive. He wants to live it through us. The life that I now live in the flesh, I live by faith in the Son of God, who loved me and gave Himself for me." You will get a handle on your relationship with Jesus Christ, when you learn how to crucify anger, bitterness, grudges, etc. You will learn this when you realize that you are struggling with anger and you nail it to the cross in your life. It is still the message of the cross that changes us. It's all the inspired Word of God. We must begin each morning by reminding ourselves that Christ is in charge of our lives today. We are going to crucify this old flesh, so that today we can exemplify the model of Jesus Christ.

You ask, "What is in this for me?" Do you know why we must crucify these fleshy desires for gluttony, pornography, selfishness, laziness, anger, etc.? It's because we *choose* to crucify these sins. We must take that feeling or desire, and spiritually nail it to cross. You say, "Why? What's the big deal? It sounds like you become a doormat; nothing more than a zombie." No, would you like to know why? When you and I choose in our spiritual relationship with Christ, to crucify anger and bitterness, God will resurrect you to a new life. Nobody can pull off a resurrection like God can! You want to find real life? Are you living for yourself? If so, it is not working. If you haven't hit that wall, you will. When you learn to die to yourself, God will work in your life. All the things you've been chasing, things that only have brought you more misery, will seem trivial. God loves you so much that He wants to give you a new and resurrected life.

Ok, I'll get personal. Twenty-six years ago, I saw a horrible epidemic of the drug culture in our local community. I prayed for God to allow us to love and help people who are addicted to drugs. Recently we found out that God has divinely placed one of the most effective rehab ministries right here in our community. Actually, I live two and a half miles from my church campus. This new rehab ministry campus is located between my house and my church! WOW! The bonus: they wanted to become ministry partners with our church! After all these years, God answered my prayer!

I remember the Great Flood of August 2016 when the Tangipahoa River rudely invaded our church facilities with two feet of water. I saw horrible devastation that would cause most churches to close their doors. In my fleshly rational, I could have said, "This church is finished." I could have given up and walked away. You know what? As a church family, we learned to die to ourselves and just look what God has done! All our church facilities have been restored and are actually in better condition than before the flood destroyed them! It has all been done debt free! God provided every one of our needs! He is faithful! He can rebuild lives! He can perform a remodel as easily as He can perform a resurrection!

You say, "I'm broke and I'm hurting." Okay, just allow God to pick up *all* the pieces; not a few of them. He can put your life back together. I've seen drug addicts who were near death submit their lives to Christ and receive Him as their Savior. Now they have joyful, effective lives. I have seen marriages that seemed to be completely destroyed become gloriously restored! Both husband and wife sat in my office, one as far on one end of the sofa as they could sit, and the other one on the other end. They have declared the marriage is over. I have seen them come to brokenness and crucify their expectations of what a marriage should be, and given time, their marriage is full of joy and serving. It has been resurrected from the dead. I have seen troubled teenagers give their lives to Christ and allow His to love to flow through their changed lives! That is the God I serve! I truly hope you know Him as your Savior. Make sure your conversion is REAL! If there is a program, system, or philosophy that works better than the "crucified life", I want to hear about it.

So, let's review. First off, forgiveness is not an option. Jesus said that if you want to be forgiven, you must forgive people who have offended you.

The second truth is that forgiving people is an act of our wills and not of our emotions. We never *emotionally feel* like forgiving someone who has caused us harm. Forgiveness is an act of our wills. We must choose to say, "I forgive."

The third reality is this: It is not within us to forgive. We must allow the forgiveness of Christ to flow through us to the offender.

Power Questions and Action Points

1. Have you tried to "forgive and forget" by using your own energy or mental disciplines?

2. How has "just get over it" worked for you?

3. Have you ever been the target of someone misplacing the blame? How did that affect you?

4. In what ways have you blamed God for your hurts?

5. Begin to envision in your mind the flowing of Christ's forgiveness through you to your offender.

6. List the occasions where you dug up the buried hatchet.

7. Has your supply of forgiving people run dry? Switch to Christ's supply.

CHAPTER 4
Make a List and Have a Meeting

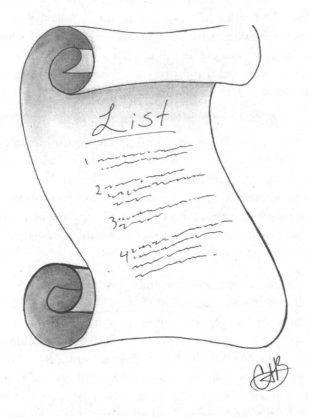

I believe one of the biggest hindrances to victorious Christian living is the lack of exercising our responsibility to forgive those who have offended us. Frankly, many people simply do not know what the Bible teaches on the subject of forgiving. *Matthew 6:14-15 NKJV, "For if you forgive men their trespasses, your heavenly Father will also forgive you. 15 But if you do not forgive men their trespasses, neither will your Father forgive your trespasses."*

Many years ago, I learned the difference between a surface problem and a root problem. People have marched into my office wanting help to overcome anger, jealousy, laziness, and you name it. The list goes on; it is endless. I have even had some who were court-appointed to seek counseling for anger management. Sometimes after a couple of sessions, and we still have not dealt with the problem of their anger. So, why we didn't we addressed the issue of anger in in the first sessions? Resolving emotional issues takes time. I let them know that my office does not have a drive through window, where I open a little window, and you state your business, followed by a quick fix on life's problems. Events that have occurred in our lives many years ago remain a part of our emotional make up. Whether it was verbal abuse, neglect, abandonment, etc., those events still play an important part in our present lives. There is a process that must be carried out in order to sort out these emotions and deal with them appropriately.

Once a gentleman sat in my office and explained to me that his dad left his family when he was a very young boy and, consequently, had no memory of him. He said he doesn't think about it, so it doesn't bother him. I asked, "Why are you sitting here for counseling then?" This gentleman had destroyed two marriages before he decided to address his problem of abandonment. So often we suppress and repress the feelings that have cause us emotional grief. Someone may give us bad advice and say that *you've got to forgive and forget.* Of course, that simple philosophy will not work.

On and on those emotional hurts continue. Jesus told us offenses would come. Feelings will be battered and bruised. I know "helicopter" and "bulldozer" parents attempt to shelter their kids to prevent them from getting those emotional hurts. We hover over them. We push away anything person or obstacle that can cause our children to become unhappy. Charlotte and I did that very thing. No one wants to see their children suffer at the hands of thoughtless bullies. However, a balance must be reached. Our children should learn from an early age to stand up for themselves. However, if we are going to live on planet Earth, Jesus said offenses would come; but woe unto those who cause the offense. We have already covered the Lord's Prayer, but let's review in this text of Matthew 6.

In this Scripture the word forgive means to untie or to send them away. If done Biblically at this point, we are released or untied from the grips of our offenders. We spoke earlier about the power of the words, *I forgive*. There is something about nailing down a point in time. We speak those words from our hearts and they come from mouths, *I forgive*. You may not have verbalized these words in a very long time. So, right now, I want you say them out loud, *I forgive*. You may think it is not that simple. You are correct. It's not! It is not *that* simple, but here is a great place to start in the forgiving process. Declare it with your mouth!

Forgiveness is an urgent topic taught by Jesus Christ. In Matthew 18:15, Jesus taught how to deal with someone who offended you. The apostle Peter was among those present. Peter's mindset was to speak first and to think later. His uncontrolled mouth caused him a lot of trouble. He seemed to be somewhat reluctant to forgive his offenders. He questioned Jesus, "How many times do I need to forgive people?" Let's address this subject again in verse 21. *"Then Peter came to Him and said, "Lord, how often shall my brother sin against me, and I forgive him? till seven times?* Now, Peter, you shouldn't ask a question and then answer it. You apparently will have the wrong answer! Peter then asks the question, *"Up to seven times?"* In the Bible, the number seven is typically used in the context of completion, closure, perfectness or maturity. Peter just assumed that seven times would get the job done. He thought he should forgive seven times because seven is a complete number. Jesus then dropped another bombshell on Peter.

Matthew 18:22, "Jesus said to him, "I do not say to you, up to seven times, but up to seventy times seven." This seems a bit absurd. Now Jesus did not teach Peter that once the person has hurt you the 491st time you are justified in smacking him upside the head. Jesus did not insinuate that at all. However, Jesus did not say to stop there. Let's back up before I get to my hub text, Matthew 5:23. Here Jesus goes even further to show us how important it is that we must forgive people. This is another amazing word picture illustrated by Jesus. It illustrates the urgency and the need for us to forgive people.

23 "Therefore if you bring your gift to the altar..." Jesus has brought money into the picture. So we ask Jesus, "How does money fit into this equation?" Money is one means Jesus uses to get our attention. If a preacher mentions the word money, everyone tunes in so they can hear every word. It was no different in Jesus' day. He taught of the importance of giving with a clear conscience. If you bring your gift to the altar, (Jesus used term "altar" but we know that today, spiritually our altar is Jesus Christ), and you realize that you have an offense against another Christian, immediate action should be taken for reconciliation to be made. As we worship God with giving of finances or as we worship Him in praise songs, an offense may come to our remembrance. At this point we must "take care of business." As a pastor, the irony of this I find to be very hilarious! Jesus' instructions were to leave your money right there on the altar, then go and be reconciled to your brother. Well, why did Jesus say leave it at the altar? Wouldn't somebody steal it? Nope. Jesus knew that if he didn't leave it there, the worshipper would be tempted to never return. I find that humorous! People will come back for money when they wouldn't return for any other reason. Often times, the absolute focus of our lives is our money! I've had church members say, "Preacher, when I win the lottery, I'm going to bring all that money to the church." I always have the same response, "No, you will not. If you had that much money we would never see you again!"

Jesus says for you leave it on the altar, but your gift is null and void until you forgive that person who has hurt us. He said go and be reconciled, and then your offering will be acceptable. Many offerings are not acceptable to God. However, I know people who've brought the strangest things to the church. But even if it is the strangest offering or a valuable offering, is worthless until you and I understand the importance of forgiving people first.

If you wonder why many people fail to get much meaning out of God's kingdom, church, or the sermons, it's because they harbor unforgiveness. God says you have a cork in your spiritual bottleneck. There is a logjam in the river of your praise because you haven't fulfilled your responsibility as a Christian and forgiven your offenders. Matthew 18:15 NKJV, Here is the most difficult hurdle of this passage: *15 "Moreover if your brother sins against you, go and tell him his fault between you and him alone."* Do NOT post it on social media: Facebook, Twitter, Instagram, or even tell everyone you see. He said when somebody has hurt you it is *your responsibility* to tell him and ONLY HIM his fault. (That is a singular verb statement which means that you are required to go alone only *one time*). Jesus said if you approach that person, tell him his fault, and if you are reconciled, you have gained a brother! What a beautiful testimony for the sake of God's kingdom!

Verses 16 and 17 illustrate how to handle the situation in the event the first meeting is unsuccessful. What if the offender thinks he is innocent of an offense? Unfortunately, the first meeting doesn't always produce reconciliation. *"But if he will not hear, then take with you one or two more, that by the mouth of two or three witnesses every word may be established. And if he refuses to hear them, tell it unto the church: but if he refuses even to hear the church, let him be to you like a heathen man and a tax collector."* Sounds pretty simple, doesn't it? The first step is to approach the offender alone, just you and him. Secondly, if he refuses to reconcile take one or two other spiritual individuals to approach the situation and make an attempt to reconcile. If no agreement is reached, then take the third step. Bring the matter before the church where, if he is found guilty, he is disassociated from the congregation. Sounds serious? IT IS! Jesus is very serious about forgiveness, and we should follow His example and His instructions. By the way, if the first step is properly implemented and covered in loving prayer, steps two and three are rarely necessary.

There have been several times over the many years of my Christian journey, God has said for me to "make my list". I must admit through the course of writing this book, there have been a couple of names and faces that God has brought to my memory. I certainly do not wish to do anything to hinder my worship and praise to the Lord. Within the course of the last few weeks, God has revealed to me that I had some homework to do. As painful as it was, I contacted those people and attempted reconciliation. Reconciliation requires action. We must make a list and have meetings!

Many years ago, Charlotte and I attended in seminar in New Orleans. The instructor spoke on this subject. He spent three hours discussing the importance of obeying the Scripture's teaching on the subject of forgiving people. Then he asked everyone to make a list, even if you just use initials. Charlotte sat next to me and she began to cry. She continued to weep bitterly throughout the remainder of that night's session. As we drove home, her crying had not subsided. She explained to me she couldn't wait any longer and asked me to find a pay phone. This was in 1976. Of course, there were no cell phones. I was able to collect enough change from the cupholder in my car to make a phone call. (I know! Young people are wondering, "What is a pay phone?" Google it!) Anyway, Charlotte had been deeply hurt by someone and she wanted to inform that person that she had forgiven him. Also, during the offense, she had retaliated, and she wanted to ask his forgiveness as well. The phone call was made. They talked for a brief moment. "Brief" is always better in these situations. She got back into the car. Unfortunately, that was one of the coldest phone calls she has ever made. The recipient of the call was as cold as ice. He did not acknowledge any wrong doing; however, he did accept her apology. She had done her part. Her obedience to God was the most important thing that took place. Her conscience had been cleared before God. The burden of guilt had been lifted. Obedience to God's command, AT THE TIME OF CONVICTION, is vital and definitely worth taking action! Please do not procrastinate. Delayed obedience is the same as disobedience.

Years ago, a couple who attended our church wanted to counsel with me. The wife began by saying, "I want you to know something, preacher. I just got saved about a month ago. I've been delivered from drugs. I've lived a rough life, and this man is my fifth husband. Now, I have a question for you. Since I am now a Christian, what am I supposed to do with him?" She pointed to the gentleman seated beside her. He listened while in shock and horror. He thought I was about to seal his destiny! At that moment I silently prayed for God to give me the correct response to her statement! "Well," I said, "Ma'am, now that you are a born-again Christian, God wants you to do with your fifth husband, what you *should* have done with the first one, or the second one, and so forth. Because of the redeeming grace of our God, all your sins have been forgiven. Now you are to obey God. He says the wife should honor her husband, pray for him, cherish him, obey him, and to follow his spiritual leadership." Suddenly this man seemed to be able to a breath again. Color that had previously drained from his face, began to return! As, we continued from there, she began to tell her story of years of abuse. I asked if she would be willing to forgive those people who had hurt her. She answered that she had no choice but to forgive them and was willing to do so. I shared with her Matthew 6:14-15. I told her I wanted her to take one week before coming back for the next meeting and to make a list of everyone who had ever hurt her.

The next week she came into my office and presented a list of twenty-seven people! As she briefly explained what they did to her, those words literally broke my heart. As I read each name, she would reply, "Sexual abuse, introduced me to heroin, pimped me out, etc." Upon nearing the end of the list, I noticed all the names were those of men. I inquired as to why she only listed men. She stated, "Oh, I didn't know you wanted me to list the women as well!" I asked her to name a woman who had hurt her. At the top of her list was her mother. She then proceeded to list seven more women. The combination of these two lists consisted of thirty-five people. I then gave her a Biblical assignment. I asked her to pray for God to orchestrate Matthew 18:15 opportunities. I asked if the first name on this list was the most prominent in her mind. She said "yes," and that he was the worst. Usually, the first one who comes to mind is the one who has caused us the most harm! They live in our frontal lobes, until we learn to forgive them. She said she hadn't seen him in fifteen years, and the last she heard about him he was somewhere in Florida. I told her we would pray right now because her assignment this week was to attempt to locate him and let him know that she is now a born-again Christian and that Christ wants her to forgive all that had taken place between them. She was not optimistic about locating him. I told her not to worry because God was going to do something, if she were willing. She agreed. She returned the next week for our next session. Her look of amazement was off the charts! She said, "Preacher, you're not going to believe this. I was pumping gas at a service station when I glanced over at the next pump and there was the man who was number one on my list, whom I thought was in Florida!" She continued, "Everything from the Word of God came rushing back over me. I quickly stopped pumping gas and walked over to him and said, 'Hi'. He looked as if he had seen a ghost! I smiled and said, 'I want to let you know I have been very angry because of all the horrible atrocities you put me though. The hurt and misery were unspeakable. I am now a born-again Christian and Jesus has forgiven me, and I want to let you know that I have forgiven you for all that you did.' I turned and walked away and finished filling up my car." Folks, I tell you, we serve an awesome God!

When we obey the Word of God, He can and will orchestrate what you and I could never imagine. We should never limit the possibilities of God's capabilities. Now, when it comes to attempting to make reconciliation, an actual conversation is the best way to make sure there is no misunderstanding concerning your intentions for reconciliation. However, a letter or even a text may be necessary at times. Written communication is a good way to make sure you include everything you desire to express. You want to clearly state your purpose. However, be general with details. You do not want your letter or text to be used against you as documentation against you, especially if you are the offender. Once I counseled a couple. She wanted a divorce and she notified him via a text message. A text? How ridiculous! Speak face to face! Become obedient. Christ says to go to him and tell him his faults. It's between you and him alone. God's perfect plan is always the best method.

You may think that you can never talk to this person because the offense was extremely traumatic. Let's consider Joshua 1. To give you a little bit of background, Moses has just died. God had given Joshua the assignment of leading Israel into battle to take over the land that had been promised them. In chapter 1, God told Israel to, "Be strong and of great courage." For you to make a phone call or confront someone, requires great courage. You may not like confrontations. Most people do not! Most avoid confrontation at all cost. Most people are *peace-at-all-costs* type persons. Unfortunately, it doesn't work like that in the real world. To think so is to live in a fantasy world. Yet when we are hurt deeply, according to the Scripture, you and I need to initiate the phone call and say, "Listen, I am not angry with you, but *we need to talk.*" Confrontation is uncomfortable, however, the freedom one receives from being obedient is immeasurable. There is confidence and courage in knowing you are doing the right thing. Bring the offense to a conclusion. Restore the relationship.

What about closure when the offender refuses to apologize? Through no fault of your own, the offender fails to see the need or even refuses to accept his portion of the blame. Let's get back to *Matthew 18:16 NKJV, "But if he will not hear, take with you one or two more, that by the mouth of two or three witnesses every word may be established."*

God still has not allowed us to put it out on social media. So, if your brother does not hear you, Jesus said to take a couple of witnesses with you. It doesn't mean you take a couple of bone-crushers or your entourage. It doesn't mean you gang up on the offender. You may question the necessity of going to this extent of meeting with people. Hold on. I am still convinced that when we purpose in our hearts to be courageous enough to confront someone who has hurt us, things happen! God moves! Actually, God is already working while we are still making plans! Have faith in The Word of God.

When God gives a direct command from scripture, you do not have to pray about it - meaning to pray about whether or not to obey. God has already spoken! For example, a born- again believer, does NOT have to pray about following the Lord in water baptism. Don't say, "Well God, I'll pray about it." Why? The Lord has plainly spoken through His Word. He will never contradict Himself simply because you "prayed" about it. You can pray about it all you want, but the answer is not going to change. Now, if you want to evoke God's blessings on the meeting, approaching God in prayer is perfectly acceptable. God wants to show you that the meeting should be covered in prayer. Rest assured that God is going to arrive before you do and is going to prepare the offender to hear from you. Remember this: *Delayed obedience is* disobedience. *Partial obedience* is still disobedience. *Altered obedience* is still disobedience. Just go to them. God will set it up. What if you call and they refuse to receive it? In that case, you have done your part. Our willingness to obey is a large part of the victory. The outcome is ultimately left up to God. Hallelujah for obedient believers!

I love the story in Genesis 50. It's about a "character" by the name of Joseph, whose brothers sold him into slavery. They had a serious case of *sibling rivalry.* I have two brothers, and we had some turbulent times as kids because we constantly fought with each other. However, if someone wanted to fight one of my brothers, the result was an additional fight because we defended each other. Sibling rivalry is sometimes brutal. However, now we are close and are the best of friends! But here is an illustration of Joseph with ten brothers who sold him into slavery! (After learning the story of Joseph, I don't think my brothers were difficult to get along with after all!) Because of jealousy, Joseph's ten older brothers sold him as a slave eventually was imprisoned in Egypt. Through a chain of providential events, Joseph became second in command in the land of Egypt. As the story progresses, guess what happens to those jealous brothers of Joseph? Galatians 6:7 NJKV "happened" to Joseph's brothers. *"Do not be deceived, God is not mocked, for whatever a man sows, that he will also reap".* That's what happened to Joseph's brothers because there was a famine in their land and their food supply depleted. When they were near starvation, they received news that there was food in Egypt. At the instruction of their father, they went into Egypt to buy food. They had no idea Joseph was in control of the storehouse. Joseph blessed his brothers with food and they walked away without him revealing his identity. After they returned home it wasn't long until their food supply was depleted and a return to Egypt was necessary. As they approached him once again, Joseph's heart was broken because they did not recognize him as their brother. He longed for the relationship to be restored and finally, he revealed himself saying, *"I am your brother."* He did not produce a list of their offenses. He simply stated, "I am your brother."

18 "Then his brothers also went and fell down before his face, and they said, "Behold, we are your servants." Joseph could have drawn his sword and justifiably taken their lives. He would have been within his jurisdiction to do just that. However, his reply of love admonished them to have no fear. *19 "Joseph said to them, "Do not be afraid, for am I in the place of God."*

Let's look at that last phrase, "for I am in the place of God." When you get in the place of God, He can enable you to forgive people. You may not want to confront someone. We read in Matthew 18 where Jesus tells us to make the effort to reconcile. God will never tell us to do something and not empower you to do it. That's the amazing God we serve! If He tells us do something, yield to Him and He will do it through you. Wow! If He is doing it through you, you will not lose!

So, Joseph said that *he is in the place of God*, then verse 20 states, *20 "But as for you"*. I don't intend to be judgmental, but obviously *they were not* in the place of God. *"You meant evil against me; but God meant it for good, in order to bring it about as it is this day, to save many people alive."* Joseph forgave his brothers, relationships were restored, and food was provided for his starving brothers and father. God used the enslaved little brother, Joseph, to save the entire Israelite nation! What happened to Joseph was very painful, but the purpose that came from this tragedy is bigger than the pain suffered by Joseph. He told his brothers, *"you meant it for evil, but God meant it for good"*. God will not tell you to do something He is not willing to do *through* you. When we attempt reconciliation and cover that conversation in prayer, He goes with us, gets there before us, and He is our strength.

Maybe you reluctantly utter the words, "I forgive." and it still hasn't worked. I dare say that the first big hurdle that you will overcome is to sit down with someone who is closest to you. Those are the easiest ones with which to begin. They love you unconditionally. You love them. Just because someone has hurt you, doesn't mean you no longer love them. Think about *Romans 5:8 NKJV, "But God demonstrates His own love toward us, in that while we were still sinners, Christ died for us."* I don't understand how God can love us. We offend Him so often! Even the very thought of our sin is offensive to Him. I promise you this: however deep and miserable the hurt is, you and I cause pain and suffering to Jesus a lot worse when we sin. We were hurt by someone who is human, and that's pretty much the way it is in life. We're imperfect. We're flawed. We are a mess and messed up people will usually mess up other people. This includes all of us. *Hurting people hurt other people.* We should strive to be more patient with those who have hurt us, knowing that we are just as human as they are. However, when God comes into the equation, you and I have hurt God much more than we could hurt anyone else or be hurt by another person.

Here is food for thought. In light of the unconditional forgiveness we have received from Christ, how could you or I neglect this important characteristic of Christ? You have been given the most powerful, dynamic truth on how to Biblically forgive. Based on the fact that God has forgiven us, it should be easy to forgive others. Forgiving and being forgiven should become our second nature.

With the writer's permission, here is a copy of a letter sent to her father only days before her wedding. You can feel the hurt and disappointment in her words.

Dear_____ ,

I am writing you this letter to express my true feelings about how your actions have affected me throughout my life. Since I can remember, I have always wondered who you were. I would always look at my friends in school and see them with their fathers and would think to myself "Where is my dad?" I would ask my mom and family members about you and they would always say to me maybe one day he will come around, or it's not your fault - it's his loss. They never once spoke one ill word about you. *They wanted me to make my own judgments, but that was easier said than done. How could I not blame myself or think that I had done something to deserve this treatment? That's how kids think!*

Once I started high school I became involved in a verbally and physically abusive relationship that lasted for four years. The main reason I allowed myself to be treated that way was because I felt as though I did not deserve any better. I would tell myself, "Your own father does not want you so why should anyone else?" My abuser also would tell me this and hold it over my head. Therefore, I settled for this abuse and kept my head down. That was until one day something inside told me that I deserve better and that I deserved love. That voice was God, and after all the years of asking, I finally listened and found my strength to end the relationship. I was finally able to start enjoying my life. Once I started to love and respect myself again a man came into my life and changed it forever. That man is going to become my husband and I could not be more grateful.

I am writing you to tell you that I forgive you. I mean it. The chains of hurt and grudges are gone and I have never felt more free in my life. I am closing this chapter in my life to start another. I will continue to pray for you every day. I wish you the best.

Love and God bless,

———————————

Suggestions for THE MEETING

#1. Cover the meeting in prayer; much prayer!

#2. When you contact the offender, make sure your tone of voice is kind and confident.

#3. When you contact the offender, get to the point and stay on point. Set a time and a place and then end the conversation.

#4. Make the meeting brief and stay on point.

#5. Make it clear to the offender, that you are on a journey of healing and God is leading you to a point of forgiving them for what they did to you.

#6. Be specific with naming the offense and make it clear that you are forgiving them for what they have done.

#7. Share the good news of the gospel of Jesus Christ. Let them know that Christ gave His life to forgive us.

#8. Be prepared, that whatever their response, you verbalize that you forgive them. Their response could be as offensive as the initial hurt. They may blame others, minimize it or turn it all back on you. Just do your part and let God work on their heart.

#9. Avoid any debate.

#10. Leave the meeting, being confident that you have done the right thing by obeying Scripture.

#11. Don't expect a WARM, FUZZY FEELING.

#12. Expect to feel drained and empty. Continue to pray for the one who has hurt you.

#13. After the meeting, retreat to a quiet place to decompress.

When working on your list, remember that forgiving people is like eating frogs. There are three rules when eating frogs! 1. Eat the big ones first. It makes the smaller ones easier to swallow. 2. Don't stare at them. Procrastination makes the task much more difficult. 3. Eat ALL of them. What we do not finish will finish us.

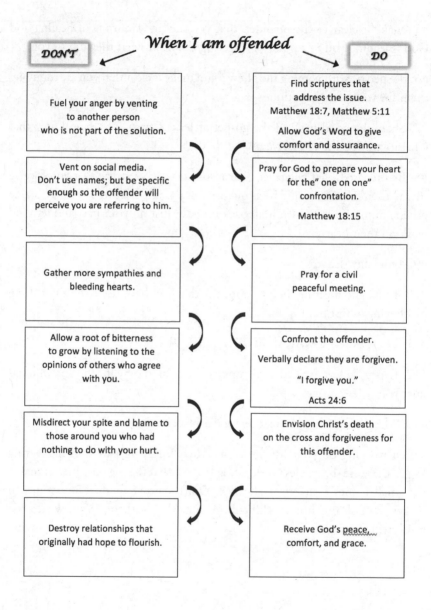

When I am offended

DON'T

Fuel your anger by venting
to another person
who is not part of the solution.

Vent on social media.
Don't use names; but be specific
enough so the offender will
perceive you are referring to him.

Gather more sympathies and
bleeding hearts.

Allow a root of bitterness
to grow by listening to the
opinions of others who agree
with you.

Misdirect your spite and blame to
those around you who had
nothing to do with your hurt.

Destroy relationships that
originally had hope to flourish.

DO

Find scriptures that
address the issue.
Matthew 18:7, Matthew 5:11

Allow God's Word to give
comfort and assuraance.

Pray for God to prepare your heart
for the" one on one"
confrontation.

Matthew 18:15

Pray for a civil
peaceful meeting.

Confront the offender.

Verbally declare they are forgiven.

"I forgive you."

Acts 24:6

Envision Christ's death
on the cross and forgiveness for
this offender.

Receive God's peace,
comfort, and grace.

Power Questions and Action Points

1. Have you committed to making a list of your offenders? If not, start now!

2. How long have you waited for your offenders to approach you with an apology?

3. Have you determined to approach your offender? How have you prayed specifically for this meeting?

4. What are the triggers that bring the offense back to the front of your mind?

5. In what way has your unforgiveness affected your love of giving? In what ways have your hurts affected your ability to trust people or to trust God?

6. When you begin to worship and praise God, does your conscience bring to mind any unforgiveness?

7. When you approach your offender, can you "check your emotions in at the door?"

8. In approaching your offender, how does trusting God for courage become your "game changer" as opposed to courage within yourself?

9. What emotions in your mind have caused you to become a "peace at all cost" or avoid any confrontation type person?

10. Write out your story of how God has arranged your path to cross with your offender? (i.e. a divine appointment)

11. Write out the three rules of eating frogs.

CHAPTER 5

Do You Want Closure or Revenge?

Unless your momma wrapped you in bubble wrap the day you were born, someone has deeply hurt you. No one is immune from having his emotions deeply wounded by another person. What do we do with it? Exactly, how do we handle this? How do we deal with it? Those hurts can range anywhere from verbal insults, physical harm or abandonment. Those offenses hurt us deeply. Maybe someone betrayed you in business and caused you financial harm.

Whatever the hurt may be, I have learned that you will not find your answers within the opinions of people. Each person you ask will give you a different opinion or option. You must see what The Word of God has to say concerning these matters.

Hebrews 10:30-31 NJKV, "For we know Him who said, "Vengeance is Mine, I will repay," says the Lord. And again, "The Lord will judge His people. It is a fearful thing to fall into the hands of the living God."

I believe there is an epidemic of sexual abuse in our culture. I have counseled hundreds of victims and their families. I have heard the depth of their despair and the extent of the damage. When someone says that they have been sexually abused, I begin our conversation with this question, "Is the person who did this to you in jail?" Often times the answer is shocking and disappointing. What really hurts is when victims say they told someone, but the abuser is a family member and therefore legal action was not taken against the perpetrator. You know what that is called? It is called double betrayal. Not only was the victim violated, but when they attempted to confide in another person, they were advised to "keep it quiet". This is wrong! That person was victimized a second time. The feeling of helplessness is compounded at this point. Don't use the excuse that the perpetrator is "family". When somebody becomes a sexual predator, they are the ones who are betraying the family, so leave them alone and get far away from them!

Occasionally, the child victim is told that nothing can be done about what has happened. Once a victim told me that if he were to tell who did this to him, his dad will kill the abuser. Let me say that you should do what is right and we will "talk dad off the roof" later. Justice must be served. The abuser must be exposed in order to prevent further crimes and abuses.

I know by personal experience what has happened in my family, and I want to say, "Only God could have kept me from getting revenge." It takes much prayer to curtail the desire to get revenge when someone we love has been molested. The feelings of anger swell up inside and the carnal nature wants to handle the matter, but God is the One who takes the matter into His hands. He will give true and final justice.

Often times, God gets the blame for these atrocities. It is very easy to say, "God, why did *You* let this happen?" As long as you blame God, you will never be able to trust Him to do what this verse says in Hebrews 10. God is the final judge, and God is going to make it right. We must not be bitter toward God. "Well God, *You* should not have let this happen." "God, where were *You* when I was being victimized?" A person with this attitude will never step out on faith and truly trust the judgment of God to settle the issue. The Scripture says, "*Vengeance is mine, I will repay.*" *says the Lord.* Now, stay with me. Stay focused. It is not karma. Long before there was ever a statue of a potbelly guy out in front of a Chinese restaurant, there was God Almighty. God knows what He is doing. He is the ultimate authority. A Christian has no business referring to it as karma. This takes away from the glory of God, and the demonstration of how miraculously our God can handle problems that are far out of our control.

As Christians, we should step away from the bitterness, the anger, and blaming God and move into a life of faith. God's Word says that He will settle the score. *Galatians 6:7* NJKV "*Do not be deceived. God is not mocked. For whatsoever a man sows, that he will also reap*". When you live with that promise, you realize that is the first step in obtaining closure to what has happened. Remember, closure doesn't come overnight, and I want to give some of you some peace of mind. *Time does not heal all wounds.* We've made that statement, and it is wrong. "In time you will get over this." Wrong. Time never heals any wounds. If this were true, you would worship and praise your watch. Time is not the important factor in this equation. Let me tell you, God heals all wounds because when God heals us, *He gets the glory* and nobody else does. You see, if I could forgive somebody in the energy of my own flesh, I would look in the mirror and think "*What a wonderful guy I am!*" However, I don't deserve the glory! I don't deserve the credit for anything. When God heals us, we are able to look at God Almighty and say, "God, *You* did this. *You* get all the glory and *You're* the reason I'm an overcomer!" What a way to live! Whatever has happened to us, God knows that one day that person who caused harm to us, is going to stand before Him. *Hebrews 9:27 NKJV "And as it is appointed unto men to die once, but after this the judgment." II Corinthians 5:10 NKJV, "For we must all appear before the judgment seat of Christ; that every one may receive the things done in his body, according to what he has done, whether good or bad." Romans 14:12 NKJV, "So then each of us shall give an account of himself to God."* We must trust the judgment of God. *Luke 12:2-4 NKJV, "For there is nothing covered, that will not be revealed, neither hidden that will not be known. Therefore, whatsoever you have spoken in dark will be heard in the light; and what you have spoken in the ear in inner rooms will be proclaimed on the housetops. And I say to you, my friends, 'Do not afraid of those who kill the body, and after that have no more that they can do.'"* You may have the opposite reaction and say, "Every dog has its day and I'm going to be so excited when that person gets what's coming to him." Anyone with this attitude has some repenting to do and should experience spiritual growth. God's capabilities are much greater than ours! Forgiving someone does not "let him or her off the hook." The offender will stand before God in judgment unless he repents.

The "gratification of closure" does not come overnight. Many years ago, when I first became a pastor, a family started attending our church. After a while, the mother came to the deacons and me and confided in us that she and her three children were being grossly and severely abused by her husband and she feared for their lives. Our deacons used a lot of wisdom and prayed about the matter. Normally, it is very difficult to get involved in domestic situations, but she presented a very good story. They thoroughly vetted and confirmed her sad story. Several of us quickly did a most difficult task: we rescued this lady and her children. I remember being there, helping her to remove a few personal belongings from the house. The neighbors taunted us. I vividly remember that taunting. I had never felt so guilty in all my life as we rescued that lady and her children out of harm's way. For over twenty years, I drove on that road and almost every time I'd pass that driveway, a little bit of guilt would haunt me. It pierced my heart like a dart. Did we do the right thing? I know she did the right thing by leaving. Secondly, she did the right thing by never going back. However, that didn't give me all the closure I needed. There must be closure somewhere. Almost twenty years later, I was connected with a young man who visited our church. He said, "Let me tell you where I grew up," and he told me. "I lived next door to that family that y'all rescued. I was the same age as her son. We played together all the time. As a ten year old boy, I remember my buddy telling me how his daddy had beaten him and I didn't believe it. Then he removed his shirt and showed me bruises, where his dad had literally taken a 2x4 board and beaten him on his back. These beatings occurred often."

I had difficulty containing myself through the conversation. I went away and wept and said, "God, closure doesn't come when I think it should or how I think it should. But God, I do know this. Doing the right thing is always the *right thing to do*. It is never right to do the wrong thing and it's never wrong to do the right thing. Feelings do not equal closure. Closure is the assurance that you have done what God has told you to do.

Just because you do what is right, doesn't necessarily mean that you get to feel right about it. If you do the right thing and you get a good feeling, it is a bonus. Most of the time we must do what is difficult to do, and the good feeling will come later. The same is true when you need to forgive someone. At the time, you may not *feel* like forgiving them. But it's not your forgiveness anyway, so therefore it didn't cost you anything. It cost the life of the very Son of God to forgive people. It doesn't cost us anything to forgive people. Jesus paid the price when He died on the cross and He has an unlimited supply of forgiveness! You must realize that one day God is going to bring about justice. The God of the Bible is the only *true God*. Biblical Christianity is the only true religion in the world. It is not about a *religion*; it's about a *relationship*. Put your faith in what God says about what is right and what is wrong and *you will win.* Victory may not be within your time frame but rest assured, God will have the victory over sin and abuse!

If you continue to hold a grudge, the same results do not apply. Recently, I received an email from a pastor who was still angry about something that happened almost twenty years ago. I attempted to minister to him. I wanted to give him sound, Biblical advice. "You must forgive this, or it will consume you." You may say, "But you don't know how much this has hurt me." Here are some quotes on forgiveness from some of my heroes.

Ray Comfort: "It should be easy to forgive others in light of our forgiveness."

Bill Brit: "I was thinking back over all the revivals meetings I have preached and one thing I have seen that sparks revival more than anything is when forgiveness is extended from one person to another within the church."

C.S. Lewis: "To be a Christian means to forgive the inexcusable in others because Christ has forgiven the inexcusable in us."

Les Brown: "Forgive anyone who has caused you pain or harm. Keep in mind that forgiving is not for others; it for your benefit. Forgiving is not forgetting. It is remembering without anger. It frees up your power, heals your body, mind, and spirit. Forgiveness opens up a pathway to a new place of peace where one can persist despite what has happened to you."

Who do we think we are? I want to go back and recap something. So often people struggle with what I call "besetting sins." They want help from the surface problems like doubt, pride, worry, fear, anger, stubbornness, laziness, complaining, gossip, guilt, apathy, critical spirit, controlling spirit, idolatry, gluttony, procrastination, or impatience. People struggle with surface problems of racism, selfishness, greed, lust, or pornography. Folks think they just can't kick it; well, it's because they are just kicking the *surface* problem. The *root* problem has not been addressed. This could be the result of prayerlessness, self-pity, leisure, materialism, complacency, jealousy, prejudices, cursing and foul language, trust issues, or boundary issues. People assume they could be better Christians if they could conquer these sins. When you learn to uproot the bitterness and keep it at bay, peace and freedom will encompass your life! You will wonder why you didn't "let it go" sooner! God has provided grace. When we realize how He views our hurts and what we've done to others, how could we withhold forgiveness from those who've hurt us? Do you think we've been perfect? Has our pride lied to us? What about making a list of those that *we* have offended? Let's look to more scriptures. These are vital to the healing process.

Proverbs 24:17-20 NKJV, "Do not rejoice when your enemy falls, and do not let your heart be glad when he stumbles; 18 Lest the Lord see it, and it displease Him, and He turn away His wrath from him. 19 Do not fret because of evildoers, nor be envious of the wicked; 20 For there will be no prospect for the evil man."

The Scripture teaches that when you and I hear of calamity coming upon those who have hurt us, we should not take pleasure in their suffering. The wrong response would be "Ha, ha. They finally got what was coming to them." Scripture teaches if you rejoice, God will see your evil rejoicing. He will turn His wrath away from that person and guess where He is going to channel that wrath? That's right – to anyone who rejoices in that person's punishment. You say, "But it feels so good to gloat." Maybe so, but that is a luxury that you and I can't afford. God says He will handle it. Who would do a better job? Our infliction of pain on them, or letting God deal with it? We must see that sin nailed to the cross, and truly desire for God's forgiveness to flow through us. The pain that you and I could possibly inflict on others will never relieve the pain that we bear. It will not make it better. Our pain must be replaced with the joy of the Lord.

Proverbs 25:21 NKJV, "If your enemy is hungry, give him bread to eat; And if he is thirsty, give him water to drink; 22 For so you will heap coals of fire on his head, and the Lord will reward you."

How do you know if you've forgiven someone? A change of heart is indicated when you have the desire to bless them and pray for them. If you were driving down the road and saw that your offender has a flat tire, would you stop and help him change it - even if it is raining? He says that if you will extend kindness to your offender, you'll "heap coals of fire on his head." Let me stop there and expound for a minute.

My dad organized Riverbend Baptist Church on the St. Bernard Highway in Violet, Louisiana. I remember a lady who attended our church. This occurred back in the 60's when physical abuse was not made public. We noticed that she would frequently have black eyes, a busted lip, and defensive wounds. Finally, she confided in my mom and dad that every time she attended our church services, her husband would beat her. In spite of the beatings, she continued to come to church! Now my mother, being a woman of the Word of God, said, "Well, have you ever tried heaping coals of fire on his head?" She said no, she had not, but she did throw some hot water on him a couple of times! Well, that certainly wasn't the correct response and certainly not what the Scripture reference meant. God does something miraculous when you and I return good for evil. We receive Gods blessings! It doesn't sound right because you and I have incorrect programming. *Matthew 5:39 NJKV,* "But *I say unto you, resist an evil person: but whoever slaps thee on thy right cheek, turn the other to him also."* I didn't say this is easy to do. Turn the other cheek, anyway!

I am very thankful that we have learned the blessing of being obedient to the prompting and teaching of The Holy Spirit concerning forgiveness. God released me from the grips of much evil.

While I was serving as pastor in Shreveport, Louisiana, a family in our church was facing financial difficulties and could no longer afford tuition for their children to be in a Christian school. Charlotte and I anonymously paid their tuition, so their kids could stay in this school. The next Sunday they came to our church and found something very minor to complain about. They wanted to meet with us. They were verbally abusive to us. It must have been the grace of God that allowed us to remain calm and keep our tempers in check. We listened to their ridiculous complaints. It was difficult to stand there and hear those obnoxious and abusive complaints about our church. They went through the entire gamut. They could barely pay their rent, but they wanted their children to remain in a Christian school and in addition to their personal demise, they were unhappy with our church. Without their knowledge, Charlotte and I paid the tuition but nevertheless, and were still the recipients of the emotions of their vile hearts.

Days later, this verse, Matthew 5:39 NKJV, jumped off the page and caught my attention. *"But I tell you not to resist an evil person; but whosoever slaps you on your right cheek, turn the other to him also."* I was reminded of the incident. I told the Lord, "God, I don't get a lot right, and I don't get it right very often, but God, I'm thankful that I got one thing right! We blessed those who had so unjustly abused us. It doesn't mean you try and restore all of that "sweet, huggy-huggy" relationship with them. It doesn't mean you are going to have them over for Thanksgiving dinner. It does mean that God gets His glory and His results when we leave the discipline up to Him! We must stay out of God's way! We must only have a desire for closure and never the desire for revenge! We can obtain closure OR revenge but never both. *James 1:20 NKJV,* *"For the wrath of man does not produce the righteousness of God."*

Power Questions and Action Points

1. In what ways did your parents or grandparents attempt to protect you from offenses? Describe "the sheltered life."

2. Were you ever a victim of double-betrayal? In what way?

3. In what ways have you sought revenge toward your offender?

FORGIVING Others

4. Have you been vindictive toward your offender and justified it within your own reasoning?

5. Have you ever silently rejoiced when hearing of calamities of your offender?

6. List any grudges you are holding.

7. In what situation did you "turn the other cheek"?

8. Now that you have forgiven your offender, what healthy boundaries have you established for a relationship with the offender?

CHAPTER 6
Misdirecting the Blame

I had no idea that this book would go this far, but I give God the credit. How to Biblically forgive people who have hurt you is a subject that has been on my heart for many years. Being hurt is inevitable. It comes in many different forms. It's always painful. Let's clear the air about your relationship with God, and what might be hindering that relationship with Him. Often, we don't understand where hurts come from and we tend to misplace the blame. Luke 17: 1-4 NKJV, *"Then He said to the disciples, "It is impossible that no offenses should come, but woe to him through whom they do come! 2 It would be better for him if a millstone were hung around his neck, and he were thrown into the sea, than that he should offend one of these little ones. 3 Take heed to yourselves. If your brother sins against you, rebuke him; and if he repents, forgive him. 4 And if he sins against you seven times in a day, and seven times in a day returns to you, saying, 'I repent,' you shall forgive him."*

The apostle said to the Lord, "Increase our faith." In our text, Jesus Christ is preparing the disciples to get tough. He is teaching them how to have skin like a rhinoceros, which is about two and a half inches thick. Life is difficult. Parents, if you want to prepare your children for life and marriage, you need to inform them that people are going to offend them. There are going to be bullies in every walk of life. Bullies on the playgrounds of grade school grow up to be the bullies in offices, construction sites, break rooms, courtrooms, etc. Our children must learn how to contend with them. The Scripture here explicitly states that it is going to happen. You cannot live in a bubble. There is no perfect job where you are guaranteed to be free from offenses. There is no perfect church where people won't hurt you. There is no perfect family where people will not hurt your feelings. *It is going to happen.* The inevitable is what Jesus is teaching. Those hurts may come in the form of verbal abuse, physical abuse, emotional abuse, abandonment, or even a cheating spouse.

Hurts may come from words of those people seemingly not so close to us, but yet it still hurts. The world is a very cruel place.

You may ask, "Why would God allow this?" We will address this issue. Why doesn't God stop these offenders? Well, Jesus said it would be better for those who do the offending to have a heavy millstone tied around their necks and for them to be cast into the sea than to offend or hurt one of these little ones. Have you ever been in the Tennessee mountains and seen old grain mills? The grinding wheel weighs several tons. Whole grain is placed underneath the wheel where it is crushed so it can be used for human consumption. A millstone such as this is what Jesus says should be tied around the neck of an offender and he should be cast into the sea. Certain death would be inevitable. So, it is better for an offender to be drowned in the sea than to be alive and inflict more harm onto people. That is very serious stuff! The painful weight of that millstone will come back to punish the person who intentionally offends people. Jesus said it would be better for you to take that massive stone and tie it around an offender's neck than for an offender to cause harm to another person. After being hurt many times myself, I began to think this was not a bad idea. That's the way to handle an offender! Let's get that millstone tied around his neck and hurry off the to the sea! What Jesus is teaching here is that judgment does not belong to you and me when we have been offended. But Jesus is saying that offenses are going to occur, and the hurt is as heavy as the millstone itself, but woe unto those who are the cause. Remember this: "hurting people" hurt other people. That is just what they do. Causing harm to others is a natural response from a person who suffering emotionally.

Verse 3 "Take heed to yourselves." Watch and guard yourselves. You and I cannot control if someone hurts us, but we can control and take heed as to how we respond. Remember this: You cannot control the direction of the wind. The wind and the storms are going to blow, but you and I can control the position of our sails. How do we respond to the wind of pain? Jesus says to take heed to yourself. Ask God to check your heart. Make sure you respond correctly. If your brother sins against you, rebuke him. Be sure that when someone offends you, that you take necessary and proper steps to approach them. The offense must be addressed.

He goes on to say that if you rebuke him, and the offender repents, the offense must be forgiven. The word repent here is a Greek word μετανοήσῃ (metanoēsē) and it simply means that he has had a change of mind. His mind was changed as a result of your confrontation with him. Forgive him. The word forgive is the word we have already discussed. It means *to untie and to set them free. Let them go.*

Someone once said there are only about ten really mean people in the world, but they have trained millions! I believe there is some validity to that! You may ask, "Why would God allow this?" That's a great question and I will attempt to answer it in this chapter. Why would God who loves me so much allow me to be hurt so deeply? We relive that offense too often in our minds. Why would God allow this? If God is a God of love, and God is the God who is in control of the world, why would He allow something so horrible, so painful happen to me? Unfortunately, I don't have all the answers. However, here is what I have observed.

In the counseling ministry of my church, I find almost seven people out of ten who walk into my office have been sexually abused. Nine out of ten young people who sit down in my office for premarital counseling have been hurt by their parents. These young people have never been shown love by example and certainly never been taught the true meaning of a Godly marriage. Parents are too busy. They are consumed with themselves rather than raising godly kids. Hurt is at an all-time epidemic, but I've got good news for you! When you and I ask God, "Why?", several things take place. First of all, you need to be as close to God as Job was.

Now remember when you read the book of Job, he asks God the question *"why?"* But God says in *Job 40: 2 NKJV, "Shall the one who contends with the Almighty correct Him? He that rebukes God, let him answer it."* To ask God the question, "why?" is not a sin. I want to refute this myth. It is not a sin to ask God *why* bad things are happening in your life. However, if you are going to ask God why this happened, you better be as close to God as Job was. If you are intimate with God, He will give you answers. However, the answers are not going to change what has happened to you. You must deal with your circumstances. If this is from a "self-inflicted wound" or as a result of something totally out of your control, God has allowed you to go through this trial for a reason. Remember, He is willing to turn your trial into a triumph for His glory!

I know a young minister whose mother took her life when he was just seventeen years old. Every night for the following three years he would read the book of Job and would ask God the question, "Why did my mother take her own life?" The Holy Spirit eventually revealed to him that he was asking the wrong question. The appropriate question was, "What now?" The Lord wanted him to focus on the healing part of the equation in order to move on with his life. The past could not be changed and the *why* was not to be revealed at that point in his life. Sometimes we are not spiritually mature enough to hear the answer to the *why* question. Our Heavenly Father knows what is best for His children. We must accept His divine authority and trust Him. Romans 8:28 NKJV, *"And we know that all work together for the good of them who love God and to those who are the called according to His purpose."*

Proverbs 3:5-6 NKJV, "Trust in the Lord with all your heart and lean not to your own understanding. In all thy ways acknowledge Him and He shall direct thy paths." We reach a new level of maturity in our relationship with Him when we change our question from *why* to *what now?* The next question should be, "What do I do with this problem. What is the next step I must take in order to have healing and closure?" Great questions! Instead of wallowing in what has happened the alternative is to search for answers. You want to ask God *why*, so let's go there for a moment. I hope this will give you some closure from the Word of God. Evil, pain, and hurt happen to us because we live in a fallen world. Look in the first book of the Bible, Genesis. Here is the account of where God created Adam and Eve. Everything is in a state of utopia! Their earthly accommodations are more than adequate. Everything is absolutely perfect! Then, when the serpent tempts Adam and Eve, they yield to that temptation, and from that point on, the course of history is changed!

Genesis 3:8-12 NKJV, "And they heard the sound of the Lord God walking in the garden in the cool of the day," It was time for their evening walk with God, *"and Adam and his wife hid themselves from the presence of the Lord God among the trees of the garden. 9 Then the Lord God called to Adam and said to him, "Where are you?"* God knew where they were. He did not ask this question so that He could learn their location. God already knew where they were and what they had done. They failed miserably. They disobeyed. They sinned! He asked them where they were, "Adam, where are you?" God phrased the question in that manner so that Adam would come to the realization of where he was.

You know where he was - in trouble! Today, God is asking you and I that same question. *Where are you?* Are you bitter over what has happened to you?

10 "So he said, "I heard Your voice in the garden, and I was afraid because I was naked; and I hid myself."

Obviously, Adam realized he was naked and made themselves clothes of fig leaves. I find this to be hilarious! As a kid, I played in fig trees in the summer time. The fig leaves were very irritating to my bare skin! Can you imagine how miserable Adam and Eve were using itchy fig leaves as clothing? *11 "And He said, "Who told you that you were naked? Have you eaten from the tree of which I commanded you that you should not eat?"* Adam made a very foolish response to God.

12 "Then the man said, "The woman whom You *gave to be with me, she gave me of the tree, and I ate."* Wow! Can you imagine that? Adam did not blame Eve, his wife. No! Adam came near blasphemy. Look very closely at Adam's reply. He said, " The woman *You* gave me! God, I blame You!" God, how can you allow so much hurt to happen? God, if you are a God of love and a God who is omnipotent and in control of everything, how did *You* let this happen?" Adam simply blamed God for his sin!

Have you ever known someone who is guilty of misdirecting the blame? Everyone else is wrong except that person. It is a sickness. Adam got the first dose of the germ - the sickness of blaming others. Can you imagine blaming God? Adam has now destroyed the garden of Eden. Everything has changed. It is at this point where people become bitter. When we've been hurt and we blame God or someone else for our sins, we allow Satan to plant the root of bitterness in our hearts. Only the loving forgiveness of Jesus Christ can remove that ugly root.

I told the story in the first chapter of this book of how I had been voted out of the first church where I served as pastor. The church was exploding in growth and everything was going great when an evil insurrection took place. The old guard who ran the church could no longer control it. Afterwards, I asked God a lot of questions. I was hurt very deeply and severely. "God, I was doing Your work. Souls were being saved and now they're not." Not long after this, the church simply died. For the following three years I asked God, *"Why?* I was taking care of *Your* business."

Would you like to know what God told me? His answer was in His Word. That is how He spoke to me. He reminded me that we live in a broken world, and yes, even in a church that is supposed to be a group of holy people. Churches have hypocrites. Jesus had one in His church. His name was Judas. Whatever could make us think our church is any different from the one Jesus started! Look around. Have YOU ever been a hypocrite? We are a broken people born with an original sin, a fallen nature. We are all born depraved.

Once a pastor counseled a couple before their wedding. He asked them dozens of questions in hopes of preparing them to be *as one* in their hearts and faith. They got to the doctrinal issues and the groom-to-be did not believe people were all *that* bad, that people were basically good. He believed that people were born good and there were only a few bad people. The prospective groom did not believe in the "original sin". The Bible says we are born in sin, and he didn't believe that. Now, the prospective bride had another opinion. She had been taught what the Bible says that people are born basically bad until Jesus comes into their lives. They simply had a difference of opinion. Now the pastor soon realized their difference of opinion was not going to ruin their marriage. It's ok, they can still have many other issues in which they can agree. He performed the wedding. After this, the pastor did not see them for twenty years. One day at Chick-Fil-A, the couple walked in with three teenaged children. He approached the couple and asked if they remember him. Oh, yes. They remembered him well. When he asked them how it was going, they filled him in with small talk. The pastor reminded the couple of the doctrinal differences they expressed in their pre-marital counseling. The husband explained to the pastor how God had changed his heart. "Now that we have three teenagers, I not only believe that people are born sinners, but I also believe that teenagers can be demon-possessed!" Of course, this gentleman was joking about teenagers, but the point remains that we are *all* born in sin. Without Christ, we are all sinners.

Well, I know this much. We live in a world where people are broken. Maybe we should be more patient with people who are just like us - badly flawed and in need of a Savior.

Why does God allow bad things to happen? Now, if you ask that question too often, it is the seedbed that will lead you to agnosticism and atheism. "Well, there must not be a God. How can there be a God when there is so much suffering?" This is where we need to be familiar with apologetics, which will answer those questions; how to defend what we believe. "There can't be a God. There is so much pain and suffering in the world, and I have had so much hurt." If that is the case, then apparently you don't believe in dentists. There must be no such thing as dentists. I mean, how can there be so much oral pain and tooth decay? Therefore, dentists do not exist! Can you identify that flawed line of reasoning? It is ridiculous to think we can blame God for the corruption of this world.

If we have false expectations of God, we will come to wrong conclusions and we will place blame on Him. Once I knew a young lady who said that she had been hurt so much that she was going to forgive God for what He allowed to happen to her. My response when I hear something so ridiculous is, "Really?" Let me tell you, that kind of thinking borders on blasphemy. We cannot blame God for what a wicked, fallen, broken world has done to us. That's absurd. This world is not fair. You would do well in life to teach your children and grandchildren that the world is not fair. People are not fair. Our bodies are not fair to us. Here is a personal illustration. For months, my nightly ritual was to eat a bowl of Blue Bell Butter Pecan ice cream topped with a lot of cherries! Then I realized I should no longer do this because my weight had spiraled out of control. My body wasn't being fair to me. I gained about twenty pounds. Now, I've lost about fifteen pounds of that, but I am telling you right now, if I could, I would eat a full gallon of that ice cream each night. But my body is not fair to me. My body should not reward me with fat just because I would like to indulge in copious amounts of Blue Bell ice cream! How ridiculous.

Well, I've got good news! The sole purpose from my heart is to stand up for my Lord God and Savior and say that in spite of a broken world, in spite of a unfair world and unfair people who hurt us, *God is fair!* God is a just, loving, and fair God. One day God is going to settle the score. Allow Him to take charge.

I believe there are missionaries, pastors, ministers, and other servants of the Lord who are trying to do God's work, but there is an invisible ceiling over them. I believe there are Christians who are trying their best to love God, but they are holding anger toward God and have never confessed it.

Years ago, I pastored a young lady who had struggles and conflicts with relationships. She had tendencies to be mean spirited and hateful to anyone who disagreed with her. I finally asked her, "Are you angry at God?" She looked at me and said, "Yes, but God can handle it." Those are dangerous words! I told her she was right. God can handle it *but you cannot*. We were not made to function with bitterness in our hearts. God did not intend for us to live in a state of anger. That is the fallen part of us; the old flesh part of us that is eventually going to die. The strange thing about bitterness is that it only poisons the container that holds it. We must constantly search our hearts and be on guard against harboring anger. Our lives are meant to be vessels of righteousness, not vessels to hold the bitter poison of anger.

Recently, I received an unusual and exciting invitation from President Donald Trump, to be honored at The White House as part of the Cajun Navy. Along with many other volunteers, I assisted in water rescues after the flooding in the Houston, Texas area as a result of Hurricane Harvey. I had been daily praying for President Trump. As I prayed for him, God would remind me how our president faced constant intimidation and ridicule from the liberal media. He paid a great price for taking a stand for many moral and social issues facing our culture. When you pray for someone, many times God will give you a scripture. So, I began to pray this scripture over the President of the United States, and I had no idea that I would be invited to meet with him in the White House. I was privileged to share this scripture with him. *Matthew 5:11 NKJV "Blessed are you when they revile and persecute you and say all kinds of evil against you falsely for My sake."* Let's stop right there. He is not perfect, as are none of us. But when they lined us up that day in the Blue Room and told us where to stand, President Trump walked in and came down the line to greet us. He said that we were the guys he had wanted to meet! We were his heroes! I thought to myself, *no* you are the president and I've wanted to meet *you*. As he came down the line, I spent only a few seconds with him. I said, "Mr. President, I want you to know that I am praying for you. I pray for you every day. A certain scripture comes to mind as I pray for you. *Matthew 5:11 NKJV, "Blessed are you when they revile and persecute you, and say all kinds of evil against you falsely ."* Let me explain something. Those who are reviling you are actually blessing you." He was encouraged! Later, in his speech, he made mention of my statement as he publicly congratulated us for the work done by The Cajun Navy.

You need to understand that people are going to say harsh things about you. People can be cruel. People who have been victims of an abusers, have the tendency to hurt other people. When someone hurls accusations against you, be cautious and make certain what they say is not true. Make sure your walk is such that no one can accuse you of wrongdoing. God expects us to live beyond reproach as much as humanly possible. However, when you are *falsely* accused or hurtful accusations are hurled at you, the offender is sending a blessing your way! Once this scripture is firmly ingrained into your heart and the devil slaps you with an offense, you can say, "Wow, that was a blessing!" Psalm 119:165 NKJV, *"Great peace have those who love Your law and nothing shall cause them to stumble."*

While at my first pastorate and going through the fire of criticism, I would frequently call my wise father. I would say, "Dad, you won't believe what they are saying about me. *Everything* I do is perceived to be wrong. Everything I attempt to do is misunderstood. Nothing I do pleases the "powers that be" in my church. These people criticize everything I do." My dad would reply, "Son, blessed are you when men shall revile you and persecute you and say all kinds of evil against you falsely for My sake." I would finally get to the point and ask, "Is there anything else you can tell me? I've got to fix the problem." Well, here is the solution. Jesus says in the next verse, *12 "Rejoice..."* Rejoice? Are you serious? Now, that doesn't make sense. How can I rejoice when I am under this degree of persecution?

Matthew 5:12. NJKV "Rejoice and be exceedingly glad, for great is your reward in heaven, for so they persecuted the prophets who were before you." So, by the way, even the prophets were persecuted. That is not new information. Don't be set back or startled if someone offends you. It is going to happen, and when they do *they are blessing you.* The next time someone says something hurtful to you and tells something that's not true, just thank them for the blessing. You think they will go, "Uh, what? What do you mean "thank you for the blessing?" It is like a backhanded compliment. If we don't learn to forgive in this manner, our unforgiven hurts will manifest themselves through anger.

People come into my office who have been court-appointed, for anger management. But there is no such thing as "anger-management." You don't *manage anger.* Unforgiven hurt will manifest itself through anger. When we forgive those who have hurt us, anger starves from malnutrition. Anger is fed through a root of bitterness; and what is bitterness? Bitterness is defined as *someone has hurt me, and I don't know what to do with it. I do not know how to mentally process this offense.* No one has ever taught us how to achieve Biblical forgiveness in the proper steps. All those steps must be in place before the healing begins. Again, bitterness is a poison that destroys it's container.

There is a strange phenomenon when it comes to bitterness. The human mind is very tricky. Those people who have hurt us are living in our subconscious minds. We then take on the same negative characterizes of the person who has caused the offense. You may say, "Oh no... not me. I will be the exception to that rule." Believe me, you will not. Little things will trigger what they did to you. The smallest of details that occur in our everyday lives, will trigger the offense in our subconscious minds. When we allow unforgiveness to fester, our offenders live rent-free in our minds. Our thoughts become consumed with that horrible person. *Our actions will result in us doing the same thing to offend someone else.* Here is an example concerning the root of bitterness. We tend go the direction in life, where we are looking. People don't drive off a highway when they are looking forward. The problem occurs when they look away from the direction in which they are traveling. Life is the same way. We must Biblically forgive, or we will become consumed with *the actions of* that person. They will occupy our thoughts. Before long we will find ourselves offending people in the exact same way we have been offended. Why? Because that is what bitterness does. Let's look in the Bible and allow it to teach us God's truth concerning the blessing of forgiveness. *Ephesians 4:26 NKJV, "Be angry, and do not sin; do not let the sun go down on your wrath."*

In the book of Exodus, the nation of Israel had been in bondage to the Egyptians for over one hundred years. They were slaves and slavery has always been condemned in the Bible. The Egyptians were deplorable to the enslaved Israelites. They were made to work in impossible situations. They brutally beat them. This is the reason Moses was forced to flee from Egypt. As result of an Egyptian beating a slave, Moses fatally wounded the Egyptian. He fled the country, so he would not be held accountable for his crime. God's people were living in a pagan land. They saw all the pagan worship rituals that broke God's heart. They no sooner got out of Egypt, crossed the Red Sea, and what do they do while Moses was on the mountain receiving the Ten Commandments? They began to act in the same manner as the Egyptians whom they so bitterly hated. Are we any different today than our enslaved fore fathers? I am not talking about those of you who have tried to forgive someone. I'm referring to someone who is hurting very deeply inside your heart. That heart is filled with hatred because the lesson of forgiveness has never been learned. He must purpose to put hatred in its rightful place – at the CROSS! You see, for God to get *Israel out of Egypt* was simply a series of miracles. No big deal for God, right? God did not have trouble getting Israel out of Egypt. The biggest challenge was trying to get *Egypt out of the Israelites*! They learned the pagan ways of the Egyptians. If you and I aren't careful, we will become emotionally tied to our offenders and mimic their wrong actions. You may think you are different, but here's a word of caution: I'm sending up a warning flare just for you! BEWARE!

You say, "I'm hurting and I'm hurting deeply, but I am not going to blame God. What do I do now?" A very wise Christian lady told her story of childhood sexual abuse. She kept the abuse bottled up inside so tightly, it almost cost her marriage and her children. The grace of God showed the error of her ways and restoration was made. She realized, as a result of what happened in her past, that she needed a have a heart that is so desperate for God that she could not be a nominal Christian. She couldn't be the average Christian and survive. (Average is the bottom of the top and the top of the bottom. Being average is miserable!) She couldn't be a cultural Christian. She needed to get into the Word of God and consume large portions of Scripture. She couldn't stand by and watch worship leaders perform on stage with all of the lights and smoke. To her, that was not worship. She needed to get alone with God and become consumed with worshipping the Almighty God. The only thing that could counter the pain in her life was to be passionately consumed with God. You and I are no different. Therefore, being a nominal Christian will not work when we've been so deeply hurt. Occasionally reading our Bible and going to a Christian concert does not work to overcome the despair.

My challenge to you is for you to realize that you want God to be a vital part of your life every day. You want Him more than your next breath of air. You will be at a place where you will be an *overcomer*. You will be victorious.

Hebrews 12:15 NKJV, *" looking carefully (diligently)... lest anyone fall short of the grace of God; lest any root of bitterness springing up cause trouble, and by this many become defiled."* Wow! A root of bitterness will defile you. So, how do you know if you are bitter? You may go for days, weeks, or months and you are okay then suddenly it flares up!

Once I had a couple in my counseling office. The lady told me that she thought her husband was *passive-aggressive*. I said, "As opposed to just being aggressive-aggressive?" Actually, we are all that way. You may be able to suppress it for a while or sweep it under the rug, but it is still there until you ask God to search your heart. I would be leading you wrongly if I only said for you to just "search your heart". When we search our own hearts, we are biased, slanted and crooked. We come away thinking that we are a good person. I try to tell Charlotte, my wife, all the time that *I am a good person*. That is the time when it is necessary to search my heart, but to really be brave and bold, and to say, "God, I am giving *You* permission to search my heart. Oh God, if there is anything there that breaks Your heart, I confess it. I repent. I turn from it." The Psalmist prayed, *Psalm 139:23-24 NKJV, "Search me, oh, God, and know my heart. Try me and know my anxieties. And see if there is any wicked way in me and lead me in the way everlasting." Jeremiah 17:9 NKJV, "The heart is deceitful above all things, and desperately wicked; who can know it?"*

Sometimes in our Christian walk, we must undertake the pain of spiritual surgery in order to rid our lives of anything that does not reflect the character of Christ. This process is often very painful but definitely worth the obedience. I don't know who you are; I don't know your story, but please allow God to search your heart. Say, "God, I am going to agree with You. Tell me if I have not forgiven someone who has hurt me; I want to do that right now. God, if You say that I am upset with You, I am going to agree with You. I am going to confess it and turn from it. I am going to repent of it right now. I want to be free from bitterness, anger, and guilt." Here is the beauty of the Gospel. We must realize that we are broken, we are sinful, and we cannot save ourselves. Our good will never outweigh our bad. Never. There is no scale with which to weigh your bad against your good. This is a serious fallacy. It has fooled thousands of people! They hope their good will outweigh their bad. *I refute that belief.* When you and I realize that we are desperate and cannot save ourselves, then and only then, we can see our need of a Savior! Praise God, there is one available. *Ephesians 2: 8-9 NJKV, "For by grace you have been saved through faith; and that not of yourselves, it is the gift of God. Not of works, lest anyone should boast."*

Power Questions and Action Points

Have you used the "scorched earth" theory or blamed everyone else for what only one person did to you?

Have innocent people who are close to you been the recipient of your wrath?

In what ways have not fully trusted God, due to Him not sparing you from offenses?

Are you still hung up on asking God, "Why?" How does this affect your prayer life?

In what way has someone misdirected blame toward you?

Are you intolerant of people who hold different opinions than yours?

In what ways do you allow issues to build up and then you explode over a trivial mishap

CHAPTER 7
Avoiding Bitterness

Luke 17:1-6 NKJV, "Then He said to the disciples, "It is impossible that no offenses should come, but woe to him through whom they do come! 2 It would be better for him if a millstone were hung around his neck, and he were thrown into the sea, than that he should offend one of these little ones. 3 Take heed to yourselves. If your brother sins against you, rebuke him; and if he repents, forgive him. 4 And if he sins against you seven times in a day, and seven times in a day returns to you, saying, 'I repent,' you shall forgive him." 5 And the disciples said to the Lord, "Increase our faith." 6 So the Lord said, "If you have faith as a mustard seed, you can say to this mulberry tree, 'Be pulled up by the roots and be planted in the sea,' and it would obey you."

Jesus explained in verse 1 that offenses are inevitable. It doesn't matter if you are a "helicopter mom, lawnmower dad, or a bulldozer big brother" who moves every obstacle that would prevent your loved one from being offended. The inevitable will happen. Jesus teaches that no matter how hard you try, offenses will occur. It may be a parent who chose drugs over you. Perhaps a parent checked out emotionally and wasn't involved in your life. Maybe it is that person who emotionally or verbally abused you. It may be that person, God forbid, who sexually abused you. In any case, *being hurt is inevitable.* You may attempt to shrink-wrap your children in bubble wrap, but you will never totally shield them from life's cruelties. You say, "Well, we do the best we can." Of course, we should. We must always attempt to guard our kids from bullies or those who physically and verbally abuse people. But the second phrase of this verse is also part of the answer. Offenses are inevitable but there are consequences to the offender. Jesus says, *"Woe..."* and the word "woe" is a stern warning. You do not want to be *that* person. We never rejoice when the offender is punished. Gratification should never be our response! When we hear that something bad has occurred in the life of our offender, our carnal minds want to rejoice. However, Jesus says that you must let God handle the punishment. Again, allow me to remind you of Jesus' teaching on the illustration of a millstone to be tied around the neck of the offender and cast him into the deepest sea.

There are occasions when the hurt is so painful that revenge seems to be the only way to obtain closure; however, revenge is *never* the answer. The pain you would inflict on the person who hurt you will never ease the pain that you feel. Never. Jesus taught the correct response.

Luke 17:3 Our first response must be for us to, *"take heed to yourselves"*. Let's look deeply inside our own hearts. He refers to a plant, a mulberry bush. The characteristic of the mulberry bush is that it has roots. Jesus is teaching that here is where you take heed to yourself. Check the root of your problem. Most couples come to my office for counseling, (one usually being dragged there against his will). The initiator wants me to "straighten out" the other spouse. The other spouse is allegedly selfish, lazy, angry, etc. The list is composed of approximately eighteen character flaws. Over my thirty-five years of pastoral counseling, I have seen eighteen surface problems. Most couples want some type of "quick fix" which would allow them to live their lives without alleviating the pain. This will not work! There are no shortcut answers. However, I want to make this promise to you. All surface problems can be addressed. They are nothing more than branches on a tree. You may think they just need pruning. The lesson being taught is: Jesus compares the act of "taking heed to yourself" with the similarity to the uprooting of a mulberry bush. *Uproot the problem.* Dealing with the surface problems will not bring the desired and permanent results you are seeking. There are three *root* problems that defile our lives.

#1. IMMORALITY The violation of moral laws, adultery, or sex outside the boundaries of marriage is called immorality. When someone is living in a lifestyle of adultery, they are inviting a mindset of dark depression. *Proverbs 13:15 NKJV, "Good understanding gains favor, but the way of the unfaithful is hard."* I have been told that the sin of adultery is the most difficult sin for a spouse to forgive. Adultery is the ultimate act of betrayal in a marriage. It's no wonder this causes emotional trauma and leads to endless pain within the marriage.

#2. GUILT Exactly, what is guilt? Guilt says that I have committed an offense and I don't know how to handle my regret. I'm constantly badgered with this awareness and self-blame for my actions. My conscience is like a blaring alarm!

#3. BITTERNESS The third root problem is bitterness. Bitterness is the emotion we experience when someone has treated us unfairly. Anger, disappointment, and resentment lingers in our hearts toward that person and continues to build over time. God is not interested in changing what is on the surface of our lives; He wants to cleanse our hearts. Having a clean heart before the Lord will automatically result in resolution of many surface problems. Is there a root of bitterness there?

Forgiveness is a matter of faith. When Jesus told His disciples they would be required to forgive, they realized, "Uh oh…, we have a faith problem." What do we mean by that? Let's go to *Hebrews* 11:1 NKJV, There is an excellent attribute of faith. *1 "Now faith"* You've read this; you've heard this, but I am not going to assume that you know it's powerful application. Let's stop here for a moment. *1 "Now faith is the substance of things hoped for, the evidence of things not seen."* Faith means you can't see it, but you have it in your hands. We cannot simply say, "You've just gotta have faith." That statement is far too general. First of all, what are you going to have faith in? Secondly, you have to have faith in an object, which is God, the Creator of the entire universe and the Author of the Bible. You must be more specific than just saying, "Ok, I'm going to put my faith in God." How? *"Faith is the substance."* Something you can hold in your hand, but you can't see it. Isn't that powerful? You may say, "No, I want all the facts. I want evidence." That is why many people refuse to come to Christ. They want evidence. "If you can show me a miracle, I'll believe." Those folks have already seen miracles and they still don't believe. "If you can answer all my questions, then I'd believe." You know what? You can answer all their questions and they still won't believe because it is a matter of their corrupt heart. The writer of Hebrews is saying that faith is the substance of things hoped for. It is a joyful anticipation of a reality that I know there is evidence that we cannot see.

Faith is taking God at His Word. This is a powerful way to live. "God, You said it and that settles it." It doesn't matter if I believe or not. The truth remains: *faith is taking God at His Word.* Take action based on what God says. His Word says that if I forgive people I will be forgiven. It takes faith to do that. It takes faith to act upon God's Word. You may still say, "I want facts." *Requiring the facts* is the absence of faith. Placing trust in your feelings is the absence of faith. Emotions are the absence of faith and the Bible says that without faith, it is impossible to please God. *Hebrews 11:6 NKJV, "But without faith it is impossible to please Him: for he that comes to God must believe that He is, and that He is a rewarded of those who diligently seek him."* If I forgive a person, how do I know he has honestly repented? His response is irrelevant. God says if you forgive the offender, *your* conscience will be clear. Faith means that I'm going to do what God has told me to do. I'm going to live by faith and not by sight. If I can see it, it is not faith. *Believing is seeing!*

Many times, we have an incorrect expectation of the offender's repentance. Our flawed thinking sounds like this, "When I see this person change, I'll forgive him." Aren't you glad God didn't do that with you? "Well, when they come to me and ask me to forgive…" You'll be waiting around until your beard drags on the ground. The Bible says for you to go to them and lovingly rebuke them. Having faith means that I'm going to do what God told me to do. Whatever the results may be, I will honor God and He promises to bless my obedience. He says for you to take heed to yourselves. Look inside. Faith will tell you that you can take God at His Word and act upon it to forgive people.

Allow me to give a personal illustration and be transparent with you. I was raised in a Christian home. It's part of the package of being a pastor's kid. They go together. However, my family had some issues. I thank God we never had any addictions in our family but there were plenty other problems. I never, ever heard my Dad use a curse word. (Believe me, my two brothers were difficult to manage. They gave him plenty of excuses to curse. But not me; I was a perfect angel). There were things that affected my life as I was growing up. As a preacher's kid I experienced a lot of envy and strife. I have seen things that *nobody* should ever see in church; and in many instances, this drama came from church people. By the way, people should attend church to worship the Lord, fellowship with believers, receive instruction and encouragement, just to name a few. Unfortunately, everyone does not have the same motive.

Once my wife, in a very loving manner said, "Honey, you have some things with which you need to deal. There are some issues in your family that you need to forgive." I remember my heart being very heavy after hearing what she said. She loves me deeply. She is not only my best cheerleader, but also my best critic. I remember making the decision to "take care of some family business."

My dad was never a person who did much listening. Attending to the thoughts and feeling of his children was not one of his strong points. If I tried to bring something before him, it was as though he was ready to pull the hammer back and blast me with a sermon. I'd say, "Dad, I just need you to listen." It was to no avail. (Thankfully, my mother was a very good listener.) I clearly remember one day I said, "Dad, you're going to listen to me this time. I'm going to talk; and YOU are going to listen." So, I pulled up a chair and sat down. *Two hours* passed very quickly. I poured out my heart. I explained that I had been raised with so much jealousy, envy, and strife; with so much criticism within my family. I explained that this is a sin, and I am going to acknowledge it, confess it, and plead for forgiveness of the Lord Jesus Christ over what has adversely affected me. I remember praying, "*This is it right here.* I'm forgiving all of this drama and I am asking *for* forgiveness for the part of it for which I am responsible. I had gotten caught up in the snare of drama and never wanted to be a part of it again. I said, "When I finish my prayer, I'm going to get up and this is my *point in time* where I have forgiven my family and I am going to *be* forgiven." I got up, folded my chair, and put it back inside the church building. This serious conversation took place at a cemetery beside my father's grave! This was the only way I felt I could get his undivided attention. At this point, I had a great visit with him. You may say, "Umm, does that really work?" It worked for me. You may need to have a heart-to-heart with someone from your past, whether that person is alive or deceased. (I do not advocate seances or any other means of communicating with the dead. This illustration was primarily for me – not for my Dad.) You may ask, "Do they really listen?" I don't know, but there is one thing I do know for sure. *I listened* and heard myself say, "I forgive." When God hears those words, "*I forgive*", He goes to work and makes powerful changes in our hearts that result in our lives being changed forever! It's done by faith. You may think it is silly to discuss these issues someone who has passed away. The world looks at everything Christians do as *silly*. However, we do this by faith. The world will never understand faith. They never will unless they come to the saving knowledge of Jesus Christ. Only then, are they able to look through the eyes of faith and obtain understanding.

Allow me to refer to the root of the mulberry bush that Jesus spoke about in Luke 17:1-6. I have learned from personal experience. Because I was raised on a farm, we uprooted many awkward trees; however, the worst "trees" I've ever had to uproot were the ones in my own heart. I wanted God to uproot my issues of unforgiveness. I wanted the root and every part of the issue taken out of my life; not just the surface of the tree removed.

Let's look at the meaning of the word *sin* in Romans 3:23 NKJV. This scripture states that we have *"all sinned and fallen short of the glory of God"*. The arrow of sinless perfection has fallen short of the glory of God. We have *all* missed the mark. We have all sinned. In other words, we are born into the fallen nature of man. Then there's a word *transgress*. To transgress means someone has trespassed. The line has been crossed. But the word *iniquity* has a different meaning. Iniquity is when a person lives in a lifestyle of sins. Living with his "pet sin" for so long it becomes his identity. That is the label he wears. So, one of the root problems is *iniquity*. When someone is so entrenched in sin, it becomes *who they are*. When we say someone is an addict, we have labeled them. By the way, Jesus Christ wants to re-label us when He comes into our lives. He wants to give us such labels as: free, liberated, a new creation, adopted, chosen, and many more! But in order for a person to obtain such freedom, the first root problem that must be dealt with is the root problem of *iniquity*. Remember, Jesus compares a mulberry bush and the characteristic of the bush is that it has a root. He says pluck it up. He doesn't say cut it off. You can chop all the weeds out of your life, but unless you pull them up by the roots, they are going to grow back.

Let's review. In Hebrews 12, the warning is issued again. The writer who is inspired by God, in verse 15 tells us to *look diligently*. These are the same words we find in Luke 17, where Jesus says to take heed of ourselves. Now he's saying look diligently. So, where do we look? Do we look around a wicked world that is going to offend us? Of course not! He is telling us to look diligently within ourselves, *"Lest anyone fall short of the grace of God. Lest any root of bitterness should spring up."* It will catch you by surprise! Bitterness is when we have left unforgiveness on the backburner and continued to live in that condition. It becomes a root, but it's also as though there is an invisible ceiling over our lives. In John Maxwell's book, *21 Irrefutable Laws of Leadership*, one of the first laws he discusses is removing the invisible ceiling. We may try, but our attempts are futile. We continue hitting our heads on something all the time, and we must suspect there is a root of bitterness holding us back. The problem is not the "invisible ceiling", but the root that pulls us back down. It pulls us back down to where we can't accomplish all that God has put us on earth to accomplish. We constantly hit the "glass ceiling" and wonder why can't we experience joy? *John 10:10 NKJV, "The thief does not come except to steal, and to kill, and to destroy. I have come that they may have life and that they may have it more abundantly."* Jesus desires the abundant life for His children! So, what is holding us back from receiving all God has for us? He wants us to have joy abundantly! I encourage you to do what the Scriptures say in verse 15. *"Look diligently."* Search your heart thoroughly. Allow God to examine your heart. There may be a root of bitterness hindering His purpose in your life. He says it causes trouble. Not only does it cause trouble, it causes many to be defiled. The word *defiled* in this text is used as an *obnoxious poison*. When we become defiled, we can even poison our own relationships.

The result of continuing a lifestyle of immorality, guilt, or bitterness is an emotionally drained life. A lifestyle of sin will leave you feeling empty and depleted. Any one of the three will cause you to struggle and will result in your being dysfunctional. Any two of these three will cause severe depression. Of course, having all three is devastating. I will cover this subject later.

I have counseled people who have had all three. They are bitter, guilt ridden, and living a life of iniquity. Many of those people, as they approach middle age in life become suicidal. Yet God stands in front of each of those people and says that He alone can remove the immorality. Christ says that He alone can remove the guilt. Christ says that He alone can get you free from bitterness. There is hope!

Bitterness is the invisible deflector of healthy relationships. Did you get that? *Bitterness is the invisible deflector of healthy relationships.* It simply means that someone has been hurt and the individual does not know how to process these feelings of anger and resentment. We are unable to change what has happened to us; however, we must change the way in which we respond to the hurt.

There are four ways to spot a bitter root. Most gardeners already know that you don't chop weeds down in your garden. You must take action by treating them at the root. You must rip the weeds up by the roots, otherwise they will continue to come back; and when they do, they are bound to bring more of their little *"weed friends"* with them. The root is very strong and is difficult to remove. It's no accident God uses the image of a weed to describe a particular sin that has a way of creeping into our hearts. That condition is called *bitterness.*

After my dad finished seminary, he returned to a farm he owned in Franklinton, Louisiana. I was about six years old at that time. In his absence, the property had not been maintained. I remember being amazed at how tall the weeds had grown. My dad borrowed a tractor from my uncle. As he drove the tractor through the tall weeds, he had to stand up on that old tractor in order to see where he was going. My dad's head was barely visible above those weeds! After hours of work he said, "Boys, if this ground will grow good weeds, it will certainly grow good grass for cattle to graze." After a few weeks, where previously tall weeds had grown, Dad had developed those pastures to grow lush, green grass! Bitterness isn't one of those obvious, flashy, *weed* sins that you can easily identify growing up above the surface of our hearts. It can be camouflaged. I call these "phew" sins. Not only do they have the rotten smell of poor character, but many times people sit in pews every Sunday, and remain bitter. They are probably not living in adultery. They may not steal or rob banks, or have other sinful behaviors, but they can slip into a church and look spiritual and righteous as they sit in the "pew". Their hearts are filled with bitterness; yet on the outside they have the appearance of being a wonderful Christian.

The author in Hebrews is clear on this subject. No matter what that seed has done in our hearts, it is going to become a weed. *Ephesians 4:31* NKJV, *"Let all bitterness, wrath, anger, clamor, and evil speaking be put away from you, with all malice."* As Christians, let me encourage you to rid your lives of these sins. I'm going to list four evidences of bitterness.

#1. Do I replay the DVD? You say, "I thought when I forgave someone that I would no longer remember it." You may think this because you have been given a false narrative. Some well-meaning person heard your story of how you've been hurt and told you that you must *forgive and forget*. Later in this book, I will explain why this is impossible. There is a valid reason why we don't forget what happened to us. However, when our mind is constantly replaying the DVD, you find the subject of "your hurt" is the main topic of all your conversations. You can be in a fast food restaurant and someone says, "good morning," and before you know it, you're spilling it all out again! Do you know why? Because it is still living first and foremost in your mind. God wants it to be moved to a different place in your mind. He doesn't necessarily want you to forget about it, but He certainly does not want you to be fixated on it! Is there a DVD that you continuously replay?

#2. Is my mouth out of control? The Bible says that from the abundance of the heart, the mouth speaks. *Luke 6:45 NKJV, "A good man out of the good treasure of his heart brings forth good; and an evil man out of the evil treasure of his heart brings forth evil: for out of the abundance of the heart his mouth speaks."* Is your mouth out of control? Romans 3: 14 ssys their mouth is full of cursing and bitterness. It is amazing how the thoughts of our minds roll right out over our tongues. How many of us wish we could take back what we just said? You cannot un-ring that bell!

Is your mouth out of control? Is your language filled with cursing? Do you constantly speak critical or harsh words? Are you a person who has no filter on what comes from your mouth? Recently, we were having dinner in an upscale restaurant in Dallas. The environment was very nice. Unfortunately, there were two guys seated at a table behind who were very loudly using foul language. Finally, a gentleman at another table spoke up and said, "Sir, I've been sitting here for one hour and I am getting tired of your dirty mouth." Needless to say, a verbal altercation was inevitable. It quickly escalated. The manager and security team were called to diffuse the situation. Words that spew from a person's mouth are the overflow of the condition of his heart. Is your mouth out of control?

#3. Am I sick? Psychologist Dr. Carsten Wrosch has studied bitterness for over fifteen years. He says, "When harbored for a long time, bitterness may forecast patterns of biological dysregulation, which is a physiological impairment that can affect metabolism, immune response, organ function, and physical diseases." Now, the writer of Hebrews never had this scientific medical information available to him. However, God was still correct when He said that people who live with bitterness will have physical consequences. There is a direct, negative affect on their health and well-being. Scientists have concluded that bitterness left unchecked interferes with the body's hormonal and immune system. Bitter people tend to have higher blood pressure and a rapid heart rate. They are much more likely to die of heart disease and other illnesses. This is medically and scientifically proven. It is amazing that medical science is finally figuring out what the Word of God already says. *Proverbs 18:14 NKJV, "The spirit of a man will sustain him in sickness, but who can bear a broken spirit?"* Acts 8:23 NKJV, Paul describes bitterness in these words: *the gall of bitterness. "For I see that you are poisoned by bitterness; (KJV, gall of bitterness) and bound by iniquity."* We must learn that Christ can heal us when we forgive other people; therefore, avoiding the demise of bitterness.

#4. Do I associate with bitter people? *I Corinthians 15:3 NKJV, "Do not be deceived: evil company corrupts good habits."* Every small town in America has a little coffee shop where a bunch of old guys get together and talk about how horrible their lives are because their lives didn't turn out the way they had expected. They rant and rave about the government, their families, and about everything else that's wrong. Sometimes, they gossip about the local church! They associate with people who are bitter. Never allow yourself to get caught up in their gossip.

You say, "Are there other evidences of bitterness?" Yes. If your closest friends tell you that you are bitter, you probably are. By the way, you *are* the average of the five people who you associate with the most. Choose your friends wisely.

I have been counseling with a fellow for a while now. Recently, he had a phone conversation with his third ex-wife. She informed him that he was a bitter person. He asked my opinion of that statement. I replied, "I think she is right." If people around can recognize that you are bitter, you might want to consider what your actions are saying. God may be using these people to indicate a character flaw in your life. You may have a pastor who knows your story, and loves you enough to speak truth into your life and lovingly inform you of your bitterness. Don't leave your church. Don't find another pastor.

Own up to it and correct the problem. Feelings of bitterness can be replaced with the love, joy, and peace that Christ offers freely to those who are willing to change.

How do we handle the realization that a lack of forgiveness has caused a root of bitterness in our lives? You must trust The Gardener, Jesus Christ. We do not have the ability within ourselves to forgive ourselves or pluck up our own roots, but Jesus Christ is the ultimate Gardener. He says that I am the Vine, and my Father is the Gardner. We must come to Christ and ask Him to forgive us for what we have done to others and to forgive others for what they have done to us. Only then, will God and God alone, pull up the bitter root. He is the Gardner, not us. John 15:1 NKJV, *"I am the true vine and my Father is the Vinedresser, (Gardener)."* So how does that work?

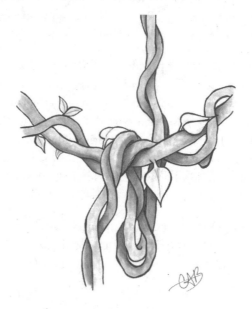

The only way to uproot bitterness in our lives is for you and I to take the sinner's place and *repent*. You may say, "But I have nothing to repent of because I wasn't the offender. I was the recipient of the offense." Really? Do you want to play that game? Do you want to sign-up for that course? Do you want to take that class? I don't think you're going to enjoy it. What happened to us is not the worst thing. It's our *response* to the offense that causes the devastation. You cannot choose the direction of the wind, but you and I

FORGIVING Others

can choose how we are going to set our sails. You can either become bitter or you can become better. You say, "I don't know how to do that." If you have become a bitter person, if you have been sabotaging relationships, if you deflect people before they even get connected with you, a closer look inside your heart must be taken and allow God to reveal any character flaws. Repent of the bitterness. No one else can repent for you. It is between you and God. An individual must repent for mishandling the offense.

I spent three years, after 1985, struggling with bitterness over what had been done to me at the first church I served as pastor. I encourage you not to allow three years to pass before you made a decision to forgive. I wouldn't prolong the act of forgiving for even three days! I wouldn't take three minutes! I would run to God and say, "God, they have hurt me, but however, I have responded incorrectly. God, I repent." *1 John 1:9 NJKV, "If we confess our sins, He is faithful and just to forgive our sin and to cleanse us from all unrighteousness."* You can't get any cleaner than the blood of Jesus Christ can make you! Your marriage may seem to have a glass ceiling over it. Don't become angry at the ceiling; be angry at the root problem and repent of it. There may be a glass ceiling over your finances to the point you feel you can never get ahead. There may be a root problem. Dig down deeply and allow God to pull up the root.

You say, "My business failed, my marriage failed, and none of this was my fault!" When couples sit in my office and have this attitude, my question is this. *"What percentage of it WAS your fault?"* You may say, "My business partner ripped me off and stole my money." Well, what percentage of that was on you? Did you enter into a partnership with an unbeliever? The Bible says do not become a partner with darkness. Maybe, you shouldn't have gone into partnership at all. You violated God's Word. What do we need to repent of? Here is the good news. When we repent, God has been waiting in the wings to forgive us. We serve a forgiving God. I am so thankful that He is a forgiving Savior. I have given Him my life because He has done the great task of forgiving me. We stand on level ground in that area. The ground is level at Calvary; the cross where Jesus died. The opportunity of forgiveness is available to everyone!

You may ask, "Well, what if I go back and play that DVD again in my mind?" Again, you must run back to *1 John 1:9 NJKV, "If we confess our sins, He is faithful and just to forgive us our sins, and to cleanse us from all unrighteousness."*

You should memorize that Scripture because when the devil reminds you of the guilt, quote this scripture out loud! Deflect those thoughts by using the power given to us by the spoken Word of God. This is what Christ did on the cross. He prayed for His Father to forgive the very ones who crucified Him! He did not silently pray a prayer asking God to forgive his murderers. He spoke those words out loud for all of mankind to hear! In order to receive forgiveness, we must have a forgiving heart and forgive those who have offended us.

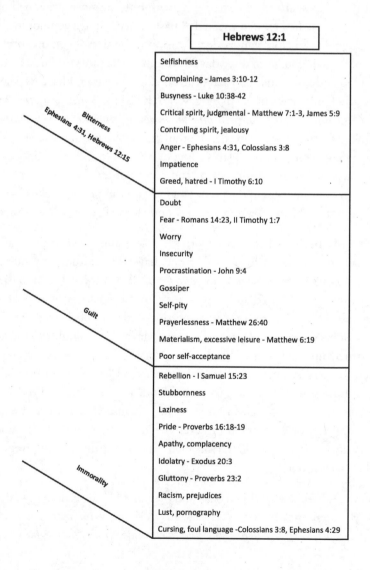

Hebrews 12:1

Selfishness

Complaining - James 3:10-12

Busyness - Luke 10:38-42

Critical spirit, judgmental - Matthew 7:1-3, James 5:9

Controlling spirit, jealousy

Anger - Ephesians 4:31, Colossians 3:8

Impatience

Greed, hatred - I Timothy 6:10

Doubt

Fear - Romans 14:23, II Timothy 1:7

Worry

Insecurity

Procrastination - John 9:4

Gossiper

Self-pity

Prayerlessness - Matthew 26:40

Materialism, excessive leisure - Matthew 6:19

Poor self-acceptance

Rebellion - I Samuel 15:23

Stubbornness

Laziness

Pride - Proverbs 16:18-19

Apathy, complacency

Idolatry - Exodus 20:3

Gluttony - Proverbs 23:2

Racism, prejudices

Lust, pornography

Cursing, foul language -Colossians 3:8, Ephesians 4:29

Ephesians 4:31, Hebrews 12:15 — Bitterness

Guilt

Immorality

Power Questions and Action Points

1. Who in your life can speak truth about your actions and you respond in peace?

2. List the 3 root problems. Which root is affecting you the most?

3. When someone confronted you about your root problem, how did you respond?

4. Has your bitterness caused any relationship to fail?

5. Do you have "trust" issues? Why?

6. Have you verbally declared, "I forgive the person who has offended me?"

7. Has the lack of forgiving someone put a glass ceiling over any possible success?

8. Does your mind trap you in self-condemnation or guilt?

9. List the 4 signs of bitterness. Check the one that is most prevalent in your life.

10. What percentage of failed relationships was your responsibility?

11. How many scriptures have you memorized to use as weapons to counteract wrong thoughts or wrong emotions?

CHAPTER 8
So, You Want More Closure?

You have no doubt been the recipient of painful words hurled at you. They came from someone who was thoughtless of the consequences of his actions. Hurt and trauma often drive us to the dark side of our personalities. This poem is a description of "deep hurt" that was written by a young lady in our church. With her permission I would like to share her thoughts. Here is her description of the heart of a person *who chooses not to forgive:*

> *"The darkness is back I thought I had locked it away, deep inside so that I could forget. Forget all the pain. Forget all the hurt. Forget all the anger. I thought I had pushed it away, out of reach, out of sight, out of mind. I thought I buried it, so that I could pretend so that I could wear the mask. But the truth is that no matter how many locks I put on it, no matter how far I pushed it away, or how deep I buried it, the darkness still comes back, rearing its ugly head, bearing its sharp teeth, slicing me with its claws killing me more each time taking a piece of my light, replacing it with dark filling me with a hurricane of emotions growing, swirling, threatening."*
>
> CORI BRUNO

That is very descriptive of how emotional pain, if not properly dealt with, can easily put us in a place of darkness. I didn't include that poem in the book to make you depressed or give any negative vibes. I will give you answers on dealing with this subject. We have all been hurt or traumatized, whether the offense was from an abandoned spouse or parent, physical, emotional, or sexual abuse, or even financial distrust. No matter what the offense was, the pain is real and will haunt us until we deal with it according to God's Word. Now allow me to give you a warning. There are people who have been grossly abused for an extended length of time. Whatever the hurt or trauma is, I have asked them to Google the definition of *Stockholm Syndrome*. *Stockholm Syndrome* is a war terminology, where prisoners of war had been manipulated and so severely brainwashed, they were convinced that their captors were honorable people with just cause and intended no harm to the captive. It is a sad state to be in when someone has *victim mentality*. It alters his life. It changes his persona. However, there is great news! When a person comes to know Jesus Christ as his Lord and Savior, he can break free from being a prisoner of war and from someone who has abused him. I have had many people say, "I have been following the instructions you're teaching/preaching. So, why haven't I gotten closure from it? Why am I still hurting?" I am going to give you what I believe is one of the most powerful answers as how to get closure from what has happened.

How do we view what has happened to us and put it in perspective? Here is the answer from the Word of God. *Philippians 1:12 NKJV, "But I want you to know, brethren, that the things which happened to me have actually turned out for the furtherance of the gospel, 13 so that it has become evident to the whole palace guard, and to all the rest, that my chains are in Christ; 14 and most of the brethren in the Lord, having become confident by my chains, are much more bold to speak the word without fear."*

Paul said, *"I would have you know"* … which means he is being emphatic. I *want* you to know! I don't think he put his finger in their faces, but he certainly was extremely forceful in saying, "I want you to know, brethren!" He is speaking here to the church at Philippi. He explains the events that transpired in his personal life. Now can you imagine? In every phrase you may ask, "What happened to Paul?" Well, for sure, we know he was beaten, stoned, whipped, imprisoned and much more. All these punishments were administered to Paul, not because he was a religious person, but because he preached the gospel of Jesus Christ. Now, if you believe in something strongly enough, you will be criticized and possibly even persecuted for the stand you take. If you firmly believe that repentance through faith in Jesus Christ is the only way to Heaven, there will be those who strongly disagree. Many people will say you need to be more like Oprah Winfrey. You should be tolerant of other views. There will be people in life who are going to become upset with you. Paul made them so angry that they attempted to kill him!

FORGIVING Others

The punishment the apostle Paul suffered was insurmountable. He speaks with the voice of experience. He tells his story. He says the things that have happened to me, actually *"turned out for the furtherance of the gospel"!* The reference to "turned out" is explained in Romans 8:28 NKJV, *"And we know that all things work together for good to those who love God, to those who are the called according to His purpose."* The terms "turned out" and "worked together" mean the end results are still coming together. The project is not yet finished.

You may say, "I don't see how in the world that the trauma, the offense, the hurt that I received could actually turn out to be good!" He says that they have turned out for the *greater purpose.* What is the *greater purpose?* It is to promote the good news of the saving grace of Jesus Christ. The Gospel is going to do more, go out further, and reach more people because of Paul's sufferings and tribulations. Now isn't this strange? You would think that when Christians are persecuted, we would "tuck our tails between our legs and run!" However, the opposite occurs. Christianity multiplies in the face of persecution. Christianity rarely ever prospers when there is a good economy. Usually Christianity thrives when times are difficult.

In Vietnam, there are two main churches: the underground church and the "licensed and owned" state church. Guess which one is experiencing the most growth? You guessed it correctly – the Christian Church. The illegal church is where you must hide to worship The True and Living God. If caught, you likely face imprisonment or worse. The church that is being persecuted is the church that is thriving. In over ninety countries in this world, it is illegal to worship The True and Living God. It is illegal for anyone to own or even read books such as you are reading now. It is illegal to pray in public or even to own a Bible in the privacy of your home! Those nations are seeing explosions of Christianity; not in the middle of economic prosperity, but in the midst of severe persecution.

Many Christians are praying for a nation-wide revival. I wonder when we petition the Lord for this, are we *willing* to pay the price to see a God-movement and a great awakening here in America where we are so prosperous. "Things" get in our way. We become focused on our material possessions and accomplishments and neglect to see the spiritual application of God's divine purpose for our lives. Paul explains the persecution, the trouble, the trauma, the hurt, the pain that has been inflicted on him, resulted in enormous movements of God! *13 "so that it has become evident to the whole palace guard,"* referring to the unsaved, the lost Roman culture. The unbelieving world is looking at us. They are waiting to see if we will stand and be "real Christians" or compromise our faith and take on the persona of "fake Christians" or a hypocrite. *"and to all the rest, that my chains are in Christ;"*

When the apostle Paul was bound and chained, he explained that the actions of the government were actually working *against* the Roman government. Their intentions were to silence the Christians. You know the result! *14 "and most of the brethren in the Lord, having become confident by my chains, are much more boldly to speak the word without fear."*

How do you encourage other people? I am going to give you the necessary steps to take in order to get closure on hurtful and offensive events in your life especially when those hurts seem to linger. How do you get closure in the middle of your tragedy?

#1 - Make a list of what you have lost. You may say, "Well, that sounds negative." No, it's part of the healing process. When someone has been sexually abused as a child, their childhood was stolen from them. That is just one of many examples. Abandonment by a parent or possibly neither biological parent was an active part of your life. I am going to step out on a limb right here. I know there are single parents doing outstanding jobs of raising their children. My heart has compassion for them. In those cases, as much as momma tries to be a great mom, (many of them *are great moms*), there is still a void in the childhood of those precious children. There is no better structure for a child to grow up than where there are two biological parents in a functional marriage. There is no better plan than that. The reality is, that there is no better plan than the one designed by God Himself. This is God's perfect and ideal image by which a child should be raised. When the plan is altered, children have been robbed of the security of a two- parent family, a father and a mother. I am going to get really honest with you. Too often, mom tries to fulfill the role of mom AND dad. We aren't designed to be both. Or, possibly the dad tries to be "Disney Dad." This leaves the mom to be the only disciplinarian. It takes both parents fulfilling their God given roles as parents.

Let's look closely. If your childhood was stolen from you, make a list of those harmful offenses and we will show you how to deal with them and to regain what the devil has stolen from you. A written list will allow you to visualize the progress you will make as you walk through the journey of forgiveness.

#2 – Realize the death of a dream. For example, you may say, "As a child, I always dreamed to be happily married." In premarital counseling, I ask this question each time. "Have you ever seen a functional marriage that you would like to pattern your marriage after?" Nine out of ten young people answer this important question, "No"! Most did not grow up in a home where their biological parents were happily married. They have never seen mutual love and respect displayed by their parents. Divorce is the death of a dream. Love lost is a type of death of a dream. A broken engagement, no matter the reason, leaves one or both individuals with shattered expectations. The inability to have children is a death of a dream that is devastating. Marriages have suffered greatly, and some have even fallen apart because one was not willing to work through this painful situation.

#3 – Realize financial loss. Make a list of what you lost. Compile this list and come to grips with this different type of loss. Financial loss affects a person in many ways, for long periods of time. Often, when a marriage breaks up, the finances are used in spiteful ways to get revenge on the other spouse. Possibly, one spouse has borrowed money unnecessarily or has carelessly made frivolous credit card purchases. Since each state has different laws dealing with the division of property and debt, a person experiencing this should seek wise counsel from an attorney and/or a financial advisor to work his way through a financial dilemma such as this. Nonetheless, direction is lost when the finances have spiraled out of control. A mess must be "cleaned up". Credit is ruined. A mountain of debt should be paid back. Once a fellow told me, after his third divorce, that he would never re-marry. He planned to find a woman whom he hates and simply *give her a house!* I think *he* was the common denominator between those three failed marriages!

You may ask, "What is fair?" Again, counsel must be sought in order to come to an amicable agreement. This type of offense requires definite steps must be taken to bring it to a conclusion and to heal the hurt. Just as other offenses, this is a process whereby action must be taken. A feeling of helplessness is experienced that overwhelms the emotions, often spilling over onto the other offenses and therefore compounding the problem.

Possibly, a business partner misappropriated funds, resulting in great financial loss. Maybe you have been fired from a job that you expected you would one day retire from and have a sufficient pension to support your golden years. There is a possibility the stock market did not meet your expectations. This list can go on and on. Your control was lost, and a sense of helplessness overwhelmed your emotions. Fear and uncertainty are in the forefront of every thought you have. But Christian, take notice! Of all these scenarios, there is not a problem too big for our Lord and Savior to handle. He is in the business of overcoming and is a master at His craft! Time is money. We exchange hours for dollars. We equate money as a block of time that we will never get back. When someone takes our money, they have stolen a portion of our lives. That is painful. God has promised to restore the years the locusts have eaten. Jo*el 2:25 – 26 NJKV, "So I will restore to you the years that the swarming locusts has eaten, the crawling locust, the consuming locust, and the chewing locust. My great army which I sent among you. You shall eat in plenty and be satisfied and praise the name of the Lord your God, Who hath dealt wondrously with you: and my people shall never be put to shame!"* What an awesome promise! What an awesome assurance!

Make a written list. Own it. The control was stolen. The ability to be intimate was lost. Respect for boundaries was lost due to trauma. *Expect* those things to be restored in your life, but do not dwell on your losses.

#4 - Realize the loss of peace of mind Then, there is the painful experience when we are robbed of our *peace of mind.* You may think, "If I could just slow my brain down, maybe I would have some peace." Make a list of what was lost and deal with it. What we think we will " take to our graves" and never tell a soul, usually "takes us *to* our graves". Neglecting to handle trauma causes trauma within itself. I am going to show you a place to file this uncertainty, so it will never haunt you again. What we refuse to face will deface us. If you want to slow down the aging process, the deterioration of your countenance, learn how to Biblically forgive people. When peace of mind comes into your soul, it will be health to your entire body.

PROVERBS 13:12 NJKV, "Hope deferred makes the heart sick; but when the desire comes, it is a tree of life". The book of Proverbs talks about *bitterness of the soul. Proverbs 17: 22, says, "A merry heart does good like a medicine but a broken spirit dries the bones."* If you are searching for a "drug" to cure your ailment, allow me to prescribe for you to *get on a regular dosage of Jesus!* A merry heart does good like a medicine. He is the drug you should be using! If you have a sense of humor, a merry heart will slow down the aging process. We all need to laugh more! Some of us take ourselves too seriously. How unfortunate for a Christian to fail to display the joy of the Lord. Everything is not as bad as we claim it is, and nothing is probably as good as we think it is. Do not be guilty of taking yourself so seriously. Remember, the attendance at your funeral will largely depend on the weather! Therefore, let us LAUGH MORE OFTEN!

#5 – Share your story. This is an important and final key. In Philippians 1, Paul gives an account of what happened to him. As a matter of fact, in several epistles he makes a list of all the tragedies and harm he endured. Why would he do that? Here is a very important key. *When you tell your story, you take back the power that was stolen.* When you help other people because of suffering you have experienced in your life, you take back the power that was stolen from you. You may say, "The trauma I have experienced is going to leave me powerless for the rest of my life!" *No, no, a thousand times no!* This is the essence of the Word of God. He reminds us of all the trouble His children experienced. God is proclaiming that He is a *God of comebacks.* The Bible is a history book of reminders. You need to tell your story over and over and over again! There are others who desperately need to hear from you. They are hungry to hear the successful results of God working in your life, even amid the trauma. Tell your story for the purpose of helping others to get closure and healing. Do not wait until your life is fully restored to begin telling your story. God uses unfinished vessels to carry healing to others.

Allow me to dispel a myth. You and I have been told that we need to forgive and forget. Let's cover that now. However, time goes by and we don't forget. Our minds play the video over and over and we ask ourselves, "Wow, what's wrong with me? I must not have forgiven that offense because I haven't forgotten it." The truth is, you would have to have brain damage in order to forget it. God allows us to remember it so that we can share with other people who are hurting and help them by sharing that offense and explaining how the grace of God has sustained us through that difficult time. If you can comprehend this, you will triumph over the devastation of what happened to you. But, if you keep it bottled up inside, you will never see the victory and peace of mind that our Heavenly Father so graciously offers to each of His children. To share our pain will then be our purpose in life. We will be able to help others and that will result in the release of our pent-up anger. Out of your pain comes your purpose. Out of your trauma comes triumph. Out of your mess comes your message. Share your personal story of victory over your pain!

I believe this new generation is going to outlive us because they are addicted to input. They want their opinion to be heard. If you don't believe me, get on social media. Everybody has an opinion. The problem is that their opinion may not always be the best view. So often we tell our stories in the wrong place. When we realize what has happened is not going to go away, and we surrender to the Lord owning us and our past, God will send people in our lives who need our help. They need answers and encouragement. Often when someone has experienced trauma similar to how you and I have been hurt, they have convinced themselves that they are the only ones experiencing this ordeal. We know this is not the case. Your story has *power*. Your testimony can give hope to others! You not only survived it - *you thrived over it*. You say, "Well, what has happened to me has made me a better person." This is not always the case. To be honest with you, *what's happened* to you is not what makes you stronger. *The manner in which you respond to the offense is what makes you a better person or can make you a bitter person.* Turn your crisis into your calling! What has happened to you must be a message to others who are going through similar situations. Sit down with them at the appropriate time and express to them that you understand how they *feel*. Tell them you have *felt* the exact same feelings. However, show them what you *found* in the Word of God. This is the message of "feel, felt, found".

Now, let's address how to take back what the devil has stolen from you. Some of you have never sought counsel in the wake of your trauma. The offense has left you with shame. That's not right! You are being selfish. You say, "But I am not worthy to teach or to share." Do not wait until you have your "act together" before you share your experiences. Have you ever read about some of the characters in the Bible? They certainly didn't have it all together.

Don't get hung up on "I'm not all that" or "I'm not all about this." You must overcome this flawed thinking. The message is about His message; not about us. The message is not about the messenger. *Life* is not about us. .

I have brought many people through a series of counseling sessions. I have given them this same key I'm giving you. Here it is: I would say there is a place for you to help people. In small group settings within your church, there is a place to tell your story. Sadly, most people never get past what I am saying right now. They never engage and connect in order to minister to others. Shame and pride go hand in hand in preventing complete and total healing. They live their lives bitterly and wounded; therefore, the healing never comes. There are teenage girls who need to be warned of the dangers of going places where they would be vulnerable to sexual predators. There's no one better than another woman, a little older, to sit down with them and say, here is what happened to me. I want to give you this warning because this could happen to you. What a great message! What an awesome opportunity to help save a life!

Maybe you have had an abortion. God will forgive you! I have great news for you. There are women's ministries where you should share your testimony of grace, forgiveness, and healing! Our God is a God of comebacks. Those women are waiting to hear from you!

One of the failures of the "older generation" is when divorced people are treated as "second class" Christians. They are not being used in Christian service because they have been divorced. This is wrong. I know of a church that implemented a policy stating a divorced individual is not allowed to sing in the choir, play the piano, or even lead in prayer. Someone should move across the road, open a church up and say, "Y'all come over here. We'll take every one of you. God loves us where we are." If you've been born again, blood-washed, and you know Jesus Christ as your Lord and Savior, there's no such thing as a "second-class" Christian. Today's church must utilize its broken members and restore believers who have a story of hope.

Now that is about as ridiculous as signing up your kid for driver's education class and asking the instructor, "Before my kid takes your class, I would like to know if you have ever been involved in an auto accident. Because if you've had a wreck, you can't teach my kid to drive." How silly is that? We do not apply that nonsense "logic" to other areas of our lives. Conquer your apprehensions and declare, "God, whatever you want me to do, I'm going to share my story." Engage in serving and helping people. You know, it may be just bringing a case of water after a natural disaster, so that somebody will sit down with you and say, "Let's talk." You have the awesome privilege to share what you've been through. A pastor friend of mine was a victim of the flood of August 2016. His home was totally destroyed by the floodwaters. He shared in his church the next Sunday, "God has allowed my house to flood, so that I can love, cry, and mourn with those whose houses flooded also." *II Corinthians 5:17 NKJV, "Therefore if anyone is in Christ, he is a new creation. Old things have passed away; behold, all things have become new."* Wow! What a way to live.

Psalms 30:11-12 NKJV, This is a praise to God. The "You" in this verse is God. *29 "You have turned for me my mourning into dancing; You have put off my sackcloth and clothed me with gladness, 12 To the end that my glory may sing praise to You and not be silent. Oh, Lord, my God, I will give thanks to You forever."*

Don't take your story to your grave. There are parents who have lost children to an untimely death. It is difficult for me to minister to those people because I have never experienced that type of devastating trauma. If you have lost a child, you can sit down with those people who've lost a child and say, "Listen, you're going to have to cling to God. Here is what I do." If you let that be your mission and ministry in life, healing will come into your life. You will dance right out of that meeting. Your soul can receive healing!

Let's revisit this passage. *Joel 2:25-27 NKJV, "So I will restore to you the years that the swarming locust has eaten, the crawling locust, the consuming locust, And the chewing locust, my great army which I sent among you. 26 You shall eat in plenty and be satisfied, and praise the name of the Lord your God, who has dealt wondrously with you; and My people shall never be put to shame. 27 Then you shall know that I am in the midst of Israel. I am the Lord your God and there is no other. My people shall never be put to shame."*

God will restore the years that the locusts have eaten. The late Dr. Frank Minireth, one of the greatest Christian psychiatrists of our generation, is in Heaven today. I have referred many of his books to people over the years.

He said that when someone has been on drugs for a long period of time, it literally kills brain cells by the thousands. He made this statement and could prove it with the Word of God. When a person decides to walk away from drug addiction, to break free and become sober, it takes approximately two years for those chemicals to no longer have an effect on his brain. He would start those former addicts on a regimen of Scripture memorization. Those brain cells which were once dead, could be brought back to life. That is Joel 2! God will restore the brain cells that the drugs have eaten!

When we minister to others the focus is taken from ourselves. Now, I know there are churches that say, "Well, you've got a tainted past." Those are the churches that also tell you that you must forgive yourself. There is no place in Scripture that says that you must forgive yourself. This is a myth. It is impossible for a person to forgive himself! The Bible is clear on this subject. Allow me to explain.

When we are overwhelmed with guilt, we don't know where to file it within our emotions. It would seem logical to desire to forgive yourself. However, even if we possessed the ability to forgive ourselves, it would be a *flawed forgiveness*. That translates into a human version of forgiveness. It leaves you filled with even more guilt. The only One who has the capability of forgiving, is the One Who paid the sin debt on the cross. Of course, only Jesus Christ can forgive! However, instead of us trying to figure out how to forgive ourselves, we must realize that when we have offended others, our conscience wells up in us and the Holy Spirit brings conviction on us. We are incapable of saying, "I forgive myself." Our correct response should be, "I am asking Christ to forgive me." If Christ has forgiven you and there has been true repentance (true repentance means we have turned from that sin), you never have to live that sinful lifestyle again. We turn from sin with repentance, because our mind has been changed about our sin. That is the result of repentance. *Romans 7:15 NJKV, "For what I am doing, I do not understand. For what I will to do, that I do not practice; but what I hate, that I do." Paul* explained: the things I once loved, I now hate; things I once hated, I now love. Christ gives us a new nature. Again, *1 John 1:9 NKJV, "If we confess our sins, He is faithful and just to forgive us our sins and to cleanse us from all unrighteousness." "If we"* the condition is on us. *"If we confess our sins,"* that's our part. *"He is faithful".* We are not faithful, but He is. *"He is faithful and just,"* which means

God is going to do the right thing. What is the right thing? *"To forgive us our sins and to cleanse us from all unrighteousness"*. You can't get any cleaner than the blood of Jesus Christ can make you! If you're marriage failed, you must take ownership of what you did wrong. When I have couples in my office for marriage counseling, I always ask this question: "What percentage of this failed marriage is on you?" It may be 5%, 2% or even 20%. Rarely ever do they say 50/50. But when you and I have sinned and violated our consciences, we must immediately run to Christ and pray for forgiveness. For born again Christians, the Bible teaches if we confess, He will cleanse us. When the blood of Jesus Christ cleanses you, my friend, you are clean! When our faith, trust, and hope are in His cleansing us, why should we bother in an exercise in futility and try to clean our own selves up? It cannot be done! But, hallelujah, thanks be to God, if when we confess, and ask Christ for forgiveness, He absolutely forgives us!

Here is the great news of exactly how He forgives. *Psalms 103:10-12 NKJV, "He has not dealt with us according to our sins, nor punished us according to our iniquities. 11 For as the heavens are high above the earth, so great is His mercy toward those who fear Him; 12 As far as the east is from the west, so far has He removed our transgressions from us"*. The moment we confess, God immediately forgives our sins and removes them as far as the east is from the west. So, why didn't He use the analogy of as far as the north is from the south? I'll tell you why. If God removes our sins as far as the north to the south, a real problem would occur. If you go south far enough, eventually you're going to start going north. There is a north pole and a south pole. Once you get to the north pole and continue traveling in the same direction, you will begin going south. So, if He would have said that I'm going to remove your sins as far as the north is from the south, you would encounter your sins again. There is no such thing as the east pole or the west pole. You can go east around the equator, (25,000 miles), and you can keep on going east and never go west again. You know why? So that you will never be able to locate your sins! We are forgiven! If we were to try to forgive ourselves, it would be a disaster! But He has removed them as far as the east is from the west, and He never, ever brings them up again. Why? Does that mean God has a bad memory? No. God never forgets anything. He simply never brings them up. This is true forgiveness!

FORGIVING Others

Do you know how you can tell if you have really forgiven someone? When they offend you again and you don't bring up the last offense; you don't refer to it, You will know in your heart you've forgiven your offenders as God forgives. You see, He never, ever brings them up again. You can sin against God and ask for forgiveness and the next few days you commit the same sin again. You ask, "God, you remember how last Tuesday…". God answers, "Nope, you confessed it. I'm not bringing it up." What an awesome God we serve! Oh, thank God I'm not required to punish myself!

We don't have to beat ourselves up. Christ took the beating on the cross. I hope you are receiving relief from guilt. If you're guilt-ridden, you're lying to yourself if you haven't repented of it. Only the blood of Jesus Christ can do this. He buried those sins in the deepest part of the sea. God puts up a sign that says NO FISHING. Please do not be guilty of taking that sign down!

If you've never had a point in time where you have repented, *now is the time!* You may never have another opportunity. God loves you so much, He is willing, if you will confess and repent and turn from any sin, He will forgive it. You can stand clean because Jesus Christ has forgiven it. Next time the devil puts a guilt trip on you, simply remind the him that there are no east and west poles. He can't find it. Oh, be sure. He will bring it up. Satan is a liar. He loves to magnify our past sins. God asks, "What sins?" Who are you going to listen to?

Satan would love to be our travel agent for a guilt trip! Do not take that trip. Yes, often the battle is within our thoughts. However, we must discern between our thought and any thought that Satan passes before our minds. Just because we have a bad thought, we shouldn't take ownership of that evil idea. We must realize, that evil thought was Satan speaking to us in "first person singular," attempting to trick us into accepting that evil thought as our own thoughts. For example: "*I* want to harm that person who has hurt me. *I* want to steal an object." Satan is too smart to tempt you with a thought of i.e. "*You* want to hurt that person: *you* want to steal an object!" Satan will phrase the evil thought as if it were *your thought*. You can't stop a bird from flying over your head, but you can prevent him from building a nest in your hair! Don't allow wrong thoughts to take up residency in your mind. Counter punch those thoughts with target scriptures; Scriptures that speak truth into the battlefield of your mind. Have key scriptures committed to memory so that upon a second's notice you can quote them. We cannot stop all thoughts. We must replace evil thoughts with truths from the Scripture. Be careful not to entertain these thoughts from Satan.

Power Questions and Action Points

1. What form of darkness remains in your life? What is feeding this darkness? i.e. music, wrong friends, entertainment, toying or playing with occult experiences, pornography, violent video games, yielding to addictions, etc.

2. What measures are you taking to associate with light? i.e. Godly friends, Christian music, small group Bible study, Biblical preaching, daily quiet time with God, serving others in ministry, clean humor, etc.

3. Have you continued to walk in the light or have you given up?

4. What are your greatest fears? What do you worry about the most?

5. Write out your story. Tell your story of victory to other hurting people! Ask God to expand your ministry of helping others who are hurting.

CHAPTER 9
Identity

It's obvious that by walking around on planet Earth, you know some people are kind, while others are not so kind. People observe us for a short while and then they "label us". Maybe it started when you were a kid; someone gave you a nickname. Have you ever been given a nickname that was something really goofy? Possibly you were degraded to the point of feeling two inches tall. Maybe, that nickname stayed with you throughout your teenage years and possibly into your adulthood. We Southerners are guilty of that quite often. You may have been small of stature and you were known as " Pee Wee". Once I knew a young man who was called Porkchop. As a young boy he loved pork chops and hence his lifelong nickname is Porkchop. Nicknames or labels can be a life-long part of our identity.

We assign" labels" to other people. I remember feeling a sense of inferiority as a kid. I had a judgmental family member. (There is one in every family.) He would say, "Boy, you ain't never gonna amount to nothing." It was that type of *label* that could haunt me for the rest of my life! Now, that's isn't correct grammar, neither is it in the best interest of a child to tell him that. As an adult, I often considered sending him photos of myself with the governor as I attended Christmas parties at the Governor's mansion or was pictured with the him while serving on the Moral and Social Committee of our convention. I considered sending my judgmental family member a copy of the picture of myself with the President of the United States in the blue room at the White House. I could have sent those photos and said, "Here is someone who will never amount to anything." It would have felt great to prove him wrong. However, here is the point: friends or family members may label you; or oftentimes, the circumstances you deal with may label you. You are not required to accept those labels. People nowadays who have just a little bit of Christianity will say, "Well, you should not judge people." To be honest with you, every one of us is somewhat judgmental. For example, a person who walks into your church, who is covered in skull and cross bone tattoos, wearing a black leather jacket, black leather pants, and black boots, etc., would be labeled as a biker. Someone wearing a big cowboy belt, hat, and boots would be labeled as a cowboy. We are guilty of labeling each other as well as wearing labels ourselves.

It's just what we do, and the world does it constantly. However, to become a born-again Christian, we still have a struggle with peeling off that old label and taking on the identity of who we are in Jesus Christ. Whatever circumstance you go through is how you are labeled. For example: In a 12-step program you are labeled as an alcoholic or an addict for the rest of your life. Let's see what The Word of God has to say about that. *II Corinthians 5:17 NKJV, "Therefore if anyone is in Christ, he is a new creation. Old things have passed away, behold all things have become new."* The word, *therefore*, is based on what you should read before you see the word therefore. *14 "For the love of Christ compels us, because we judge thus: that if One died for all, then all died; 15 and He died for all, that those who live should live no longer for themselves...."*.

Now, there's part of our identity. We are not selfish. *"But for Him who died for them and rose again".* There's the gospel. *16 "Therefore, from now on, we regard no one according to the flesh. Even though we have known Christ according to the flesh, yet, now we know Him thus no longer; 17 Therefore, for anyone is in Christ he is a new creation. Old things have passed away, behold all things have become new".*

We just read the word *therefore*. Then the writer, Paul, uses the word, *if*. IF is a big word! The Bible uses that word frequently. It's conditional. Someone once said that life takes place between the i and f of the word *if*. There is much truth in that statement. *If* is conditional. It is defined as when certain predetermined conditions are met. Christ will never violate your will in order to be a part of your life. You must *if,* "conditionally" repent of sin and choose to receive Christ as your Lord and Savior. God is never going to force His salvation on anyone. However, anyone who repents of sin has a new identity as being "in Christ." This becomes your new identity. If you look up every time the Bible refers to being "in Christ," you will find that is the identity of a born-again believer. We are in Christ and Christ is in us. We become consumed with Christ after having the born again experience. He is in us and we're in Him. He says, *if,* "conditionally", if anyone is in Christ, simply means he is a new creation. You became brand new and the new creation becomes your identity. It is a position that becomes your "brand"! This brand defines and depicts our purpose.

Never allow your past OR the opinions of others to define you. When you are born again, you are an "ex" whatever you were. That's why twelve step programs are not effective. They leave you in bondage by saying you will always be an addict. If a new creature is a *new creature*, the Bible says that old things are passed away. That's shouting ground for those of us who really get a hold of this! At the very least, it should put a smile on our faces to realize that we're not what we used to be! Praise God! I'm not what I used to be, I'm not what I'm going to be, but, praise God I'm not what I was! By the way, the world is never going to forget who you were before you got saved. Your family may never forget who you were, but Jesus does "forget" and His opinion is all that matters! Praise the Lord! Never let your past define who you are. When you are born again, you are an "ex" whatever you used to be! Your identity is no longer in an addiction or flaw. *I Corinthians 6:ll NKJV, "And such were some of you; but You were washed, but you were sanctified, but you were justified in the name of the Lord Jesus, and by the Spirit of our God."*

Another label we wear is that of our vocation. We may identify as a plumber, doctor, electrician, welder, pilot, preacher, teacher, or a supervisor. This list is endless. Whatever your profession may be, it is problematic to allow it to determine your identity. When you reach the point in your life where you can no longer do that job you will have lost your identity. You were mislabeled. Unless you die early, you will probably retire from your vocation and no longer be able to perform that vocation. How will you identify yourself at that point in your life? I know this: when I realize who I am in Christ, my identity is changed. I am now a child of the King! When my job description changes from "pastor" to "retired pastor," my identity in Christ will remain the same! For the average man, retirement means getting paroled to his wife. Now the wife has *more husband* and *less money*, and now his main purpose in life is operating the riding lawn mower and the weed eater. He feels as though he is at a loss of who he really is because he may have overseen a department of a company or may have been manager of large corporation and now he realizes he no longer knows *who he is.* Here is the problem.

If you place your identity in your profession, and you change your occupation, you will continue to be who you are, because you're a born-again Child of

God! That fact will never change. You see, it is shallow thinking when we identify ourselves by what we do in this life. Our eternal life is far more important.

You may want to identify as husband or a wife. Hold on a minute. Divorce can happen, God forbid. Your spouse may pass away. If you know who you are in Christ, your marital status will not define you. By the way, many single people don't know how to identify and be happy as a single person, so therefore when they do marry, many times the marriage is not successful. Before you can learn how to be married, you must know who you are in Christ as a single individual. Be dependent on God and only God to be your identity. It is then that you are ready to be joined with your spouse in marriage. The only thing worse than being single and alone is to be married and alone. Most people are not ready to be married because they've never learned who they are as an individual, a single person.

If you place your identity as a born-again believer in Christ, that fact never changes. I remember back in the 1970's a great preacher recorded a sermon. It was an exciting sermon that helped change my life. It came out on a 33 ⅓ record. (For all young people, that is a big black CD - for lack of a better term). Vance Havner preached a sermon entitled *Being Who You Have Become.* He brought out this very truth that when you see who you are in Jesus Christ, you're not trying to act better, you should be *who you have already become.* That sermon changed how I view my relationship with Christ. I realized that I don't have to try to fit into a mold that is designed by the church or fit into a mold that people expect of me. I'm already molded in Jesus Christ. I don't have to try to do better. I must let the One living inside of me be the Ruler my life. You may use the excuse, "I'm just hung up with this sin in my life." That is, in fact, just an excuse. An excuse is "the skin of a reason stuffed full of a lie." When you live out the person of Jesus Christ you'll become more like Him. He is the perfect model. He is the perfect identity.

You see, when you are born again, sin is still present, but it's not preeminent. Our sinful nature is no longer our identity. It's the lifestyle we have learned to hate because our identities have been changed.

Do you remember the Old Testament story when King David took over the kingdom after Saul died? Saul's son, Jonathan, fathered a little boy named

Mephibosheth. When he was just a baby, the enemy came to drive his family out of town. In the nurse's attempt to flee, she dropped Mephibosheth and his legs were broken due to the fall. He was crippled for the remainder of his life. He lived in a town called Lo-debar where he was labeled as a cripple and a refugee. After Saul's death, David was anointed King and he wanted to do right by his enemies. He asked the governors, "Is there anyone still alive who is a descendant of Saul?" (That horrible king who tried to kill David in most of his early life). One of the governors informed him of Mephibosheth who lived in Lo-debar. The town was known as the slums; it was less than the ghettos. King David sent governors down to Lo-debar to retrieve him out of the slums. No longer did Mephibosheth eat from the garbage dump of the city but was brought to live in the king's palace. He sat at the king's table for the rest of his life. This story is found in II Samuel 4:4 and II Samuel 9:1-13.

I have great news for you! That is precisely what Jesus Christ did for us. We lived down in the slums of Lo-debar. We were spiritually crippled. We begged for crumbs and the King of Kings and Lord of Lords came and rescued us! Now we are part of the family feasting at the king's table. We no longer feed from the world's garbage dump! *Praise the Lord!* Mephibosheth never, ever went back to the slums of Lo-debar. So, who are we?

Is your label a "mental health issue"? Mental health providers do everything in their power to enable us to function with normal, happy, healthy lives. If you suffer from depression, don't fall into the snare or temptation to allow depression to become your label. You may struggle with depression, but that's not your identity. There's a difference. You may be labeled as bipolar, but that's not who you are. It is possible for born again believers to struggle with mental health issues. I'm not of the religion that believes that being possessed by the devil is always the source of depression. It may label your battle ground but don't allow it to label your identity! If you are a born-again believer, Satan is outside of you; not inside you. Christ lives inside you! There's a difference. We've already read in II Corinthians that you are a new creation. In Acts 11:26 NKJV, the disciples were labeled as Christians. *26 "And when he had found him, he brought him to Antioch. So, it was that for a whole year they assembled with the church and taught a great many people. And the disciples were first called Christians in Antioch."*

The word Christian was used as a nickname in order to slander all believers. They were called "little Jesuses". Let me say, every time the world and the religious crowd attempt to pin a bad label on us, Jesus turns it into something positive. Go ahead and call us *little Jesuses*. Thank you for the compliment!

Have you ever been the victim of a backhanded compliment? "You must be one of those Christians!" Smile, and say, "Thanks for the compliment." "You're one of those Jesus freaks." Smile. Thank you so much. I appreciate the compliment." They meant it to be unkind, but we receive it for God's glory. Allow people to label you as we're labeled by as the Word of God, *Christians!*

Hey, Mephibosheth! You're no longer a child of a reprobate; you are a child of the King! Now we are called the children of God! Something or someone may have tragically altered your childhood. Possibly, there was a crisis; abuse was inevitable. In any case, something may be missing from your childhood. I have great news for you! You can relive your childhood! When you are born again, God allows you to become totally dependent on Him, just as a child is totally dependent on his father and mother. God wants you to be dependent on Him as your heavenly Father. He will never abandon you. He will always provide for you, and protect you. *Deuteronomy 31:6 NKJV, "Be strong and of good courage, do not fear nor be afraid of them; for the Lord your God, He is the One who goes with you. He will not leave you nor forsake you." Hebrews 13:5 NKJV, "Let your conduct be without covetousness; and be content with such things as ye have. For He Himself has said, I will never leave you no forsake you."* You can go back and be a kid again, when you are a child of God. Isn't that great news? *You're a child of God!* Now begin living within your privilege! Anything less than this position would be living beneath your privilege. When you realize you're a child of God, you don't go slopping at hog pens ever again! You eat from the King's table. Praise the Lord, you're a Child of God. You're a new creation. *1 Peter 2:9 NKJV, "But you are a chosen generation, a royal priesthood, a holy nation. His own special people, that you may proclaim the praises of Him who called you out of darkness into His marvelous light!"*

I love the fun we have had with this chapter. This is spiritual fun. *1 Peter 2. " But you're a chosen generation".* You were selected! Somebody chose *you.* Allow your mind to become saturated with what God says about *you!* Allow me to repeat myself: You are chosen, selected, picked! As a child my older brother teased me. He constantly told me that I was adopted. This broke my heart! In a moment of courage and boldness I approached my father and said, "Dad, I don't look like my brothers and sister. Dad, was I adopted?" I was surprised at his reply. He said, "No, son. You were not adopted. Adoption means we would have picked you and we would have *never picked you.*" Yeah, that's funny when I tell it and I've told it one thousand times before! Seriously, take heed. *YOU ARE A CHILD OF GOD!* Live like it. You're a chosen generation; you're a royal priesthood, a Holy nation. The new King James calls us a *special people*; the old King James refers to us as a *peculiar people.* Hallelujah, we're peculiar. The Lord labels us as peculiar, as in, we don't have to live like the world. This news keeps getting better. You're a peculiar people; a special people that you should proclaim the praises of Him, who has called you out of darkness into His marvelous light!

There are two other identities you have as a Christian. One is *salt* and the other is *light.* Let's examine this scripture. You are salt because salt preserves. *Matthew 5: 13-14 NJKV, "You are the salt of the earth; but if the salt loses its flavor, how shall it be seasoned? It is then good for nothing, but to be thrown out and trampled underfoot by men. You are the light of the world. A city that is set on a hill cannot be hidden."*

We were in Iowa recently and there had been huge snowstorm. A thick blanket of snow covered everything! So, salt is used on streets and sidewalks to help melt the ice and snow. Now, upon entering my daughter's home, she demands that everyone remove his shoes. I could never understand why she required this of every houseguest. Finally, it occurred to me that walking through ice and snow, your shoes become thick with salt and if salt is brought into a home, it can destroy floor coverings. Salt is powerful. Ice will literally melt, when the temperature is still below freezing. Let me tell you, there's coldness in this world. There is a spiritual coldness and God wants us to be His salt! When the world is freezing cold spiritually, you and I can be used to melt the ice and making it safe to move around. Wow! Salt can melt frozen hearts. *We are His salt.*

We are His light. We're in a dark place. Everywhere you turn, you can clearly see the darkness of Satan is being promoted. But you know what we're to do? He said we are light. We are Salt and Light. *Romans 8:37 NJKV, "Yet in all these things, we are more than conquerors through Him who loved us."* Here's the definition of our identity: *more than conquerors.* We are not just conquerors, we are *more*. Here is the Biblical picture that comes with those words, "more than conquerors". Remember when David, the little teenage boy, slew Goliath? Great story, true story. Remember most of the time when the story is told, it usually ends when David slings the rock, hits Goliath in the forehead, and Goliath hits the ground. The continuation of the story becomes a little more graphic and not necessarily suitable for children's Bible class. When David slew Goliath with the help of God's power, David picked up Goliath's sword. Goliath was over ten feet tall, so this sword was most likely longer that David was tall. He not only conquered Goliath, he used Goliath's sword to cut off the giant's head. David could have stopped after seeing Goliath lying dead on the ground, but he did not. No, David was more than a conqueror! He took the head of Goliath and went back into the city. The Scriptures verify this story. David took the decapitated head and ran up and down the streets of Jerusalem. Women sang songs while David spent the rest of the day carrying a bloody head of a giant through the city streets. He was proud of his trophy. But I tell you, David celebrated God's victory. He conquered! That's the picture. When you and I are in a spiritual battle, we not only conquered our sin, we overcame it. We are more than conquerors.

When we come to the realization that Jesus Christ has already conquered death, hell, the grave and sin, we live with *His identity* and not ours. Don't ever allow your circumstances to identify who you are. Don't ever let your past identify you. Be more than a conqueror! According to Romans 10:13, we are *saved*. We never can get our brains spiritually wrapped around "saved" until we realize how *lost* we really were!

In 2004, I was diagnosed with a cancerous tumor attached to my thyroid. After surgery and radiation treatment, I am not a cancer survivor! *I am a cancer overcomer*! *I am a cancer conqueror*! We Christians should not live our lives as victims. We are overcomers of Satan and sin!

My daughter and I once attended a Father/Daughter retreat at J.H. Ranch in northern California. It was one of the most beautiful places we've ever visited. We had a great week, but I remember one night while attempting to return to the lodge, I wandered off the main path and got lost. It was dark, very dark. I'd put my hand in front of my face and I couldn't even see it because it because of the darkness. While stumbling down the path, occasionally I could hear the sounds of laughter coming from the lodge. I determined that I would walk straight toward the sounds. Eventually, I found my way through the woods and back to the lodge.

Being lost is a miserable state. You can never appreciate being saved until you know how lost you were spiritually. We're saved. We're adopted. We're flawless.

Allow me to give you several points concerning our identities: First point: **Our label or our identity must describe our purpose in life.** Jesus called us ambassadors. He called us witnesses. Your sole purpose is for your life to bring honor and glory to God. Plus nothing, minus nothing.

Second point: **The mystery of our identity is hidden in the mystery of Jesus Christ.** Christ did not come to be served, but to serve. *Matthew 20:28 NKJV, "Just as the Son of Man came not to be served,, but to serve, and to give His life a ransom for many."*

Christ was righteous. You and I have no righteousness within us. At the point of salvation, He comes into our lives and *He* becomes our righteousness. We stand before God, flawless and righteous, not because our good outweighed our bad but because God can no longer view you and I as sinners. He looks at us through the person of His Son, Jesus Christ who took our place on the cross. God has been good to us. It is a small thing for us to give Him our lives, solely and wholeheartedly. He has given us breath, air, water, food, and all of life's necessities. We owe Him our lives. We have been bought with a price, the blood of Jesus Christ. So, the mystery of our identity is not easy to find. Most people never find it. One of the heartbreaks of life is when folks never find their purpose. Sadder than that is a person who claims to be born again and never finds his true purpose or destiny. This is because it is in the mystery of who Jesus Christ is, and when He consumes us, He reveals our purpose and our identity. *Mark 10:45NKJV, "For even the Son of Man did not come to be served, but to serve, and to give His life a ransom for many."*

Third point: Stop trying to do better. Start being whom you have become. Be who you are in Christ Jesus. "Well, I'm trying" is a cop-out expression. It's a cop-out for when we mess up or when we sin. "Well, I'm trying to do better." I'm telling you that we use this as an alibi by saying, "I'm just human" as if we had to tell people. "Well, I just mess up." "I'm just an old sinner saved by grace." Never put the emphasis on "the old sinner". That is no longer our identity. We are saved. I was a *wretch* before I because a Christian, but thank God for Jesus Christ. *I am now an ex-wretch.* This is good news, isn't it? Now, don't get me wrong, we need to remember what we were, so we can appreciate who we are now in Christ. Remember, our identity has changed. Stop trying to act better. "Well, preacher… we're going to try and get in church." Just become who you are in Christ, and you will be *drawn* to the church. *Ephesians 5:25 NKJV, "Husbands, love your wives, just as Christ also loved the church, and gave himself for her."* Be who you are in Christ and you will be drawn to spend time in the Word of God. Realize who you are in Christ and those old habits will peel away. They will fall by the wayside. Remember, Mephibosheth no longer ate at a garbage dump down in Lo-debar. He moved up to the kings table! You too are a child of the King! We have been forgiven and we are people who forgive other people.

Our life assignment is in our identity. We are to walk with God and share the gospel with others. We are to help other people come to know Christ. Our assignment in life is for our lives to bring honor and glory to God. Let *that* be who we are. *Acts 1:8 NKJV, "But you shall receive power when the Holy Spirit has come upon you, and you shall be witnesses to me in Jerusalem, and in all Judea and Samaria, and to the end of the earth."* That *is* who we are.

As you conclude the reading of this book, my prayer is that you have found total forgiveness through the grace of our Lord and Savior and a better understanding of the character of God the Father. The journey of healing has begun!

Power Question and Action Points

1. What nickname or label has been placed on you?

2. Do you believe people can change? Do you believe you can change?

3. What steps have you taken to exemplify your new identity as a Christian?

4. In what ways have you broken free of your past?

5. What generational sins have you acknowledged and claimed forgiveness?

6. What generational curses have you broken in order to free up your descendants? (i.e. battles your children will never face)

7. As a Christian, what is your favorite, new label?

8. As a Christian, write down the sole purpose of your life.

9. What are your "Ex" or former labels?

CHAPTER 10
The Million Dollar Question, What Is It?

In your opinion, what is required for a person to get into Heaven? Your answer may sound something like this, "You must be a good person."

My next question is: So, do you consider yourself to be a good person? You may answer, "Yes." So how do you define *a good person*? You may say being a good person means, to be good to others, be honest, keep the commandments, do good deeds, or keep the sacraments. So, would you be willing to "take the good person test?" All I ask is that you be totally honest with yourself.

Question 1: Have you ever told a lie? Have you ever exaggerated the truth?
Response: What do you call a person who tells lies?
Answer: A liar

Question 2: Have you ever taken anything that did not belong to you no matter it's value? (i.e., download music or movies without paying?)
Response: What do you call a person who takes something that does not belong to him?
Answer: A thief

Question 3: Have you ever committed adultery? No? Jesus said if you have looked at someone with a lustful thought, sexual desire, that is sin and adultery of the heart.
Response: What do you call someone who commits adultery?
Answer: An adulterer

Question 4: Have you ever used God's name in vain? (i.e. OMG) Or used it as a four letter, filth word to express disgust? That is called blasphemy and the Bible says all liars, thieves, and blasphemers will have their part in the lake of fire.

Response: What do you call someone who blasphemes?
Answer: A blasphemer

Question 5: Have you ever broken the fifth commandment of disrespecting your parents? James 2:10 NKJV, *"For whoever shall keep the whole law, and yet stumble in one point, he is guilty of all."*

I'm not your judge but by your own admission, you are a lying, thieving, blasphemous, adulterer at heart, who has dishonored your parents. For these sins, you must face God on the day of judgment. I have very bad news for you. You are just like the rest of us. You are NOT a good person. *Jeremiah 17:9 NKJV, "The heart is deceitful above all things, and desperately wicked: who can know it?" Romans 3:10. "As it is written, there is none righteous, no, not one."*

If you were to die today and you stood in God's courtroom, would He find you innocent or guilty of breaking His laws? You would be found GUILTY! So, should God reward you by allowing you to enter Heaven or should He punish you and send you to Hell? How should you be judged? God, the Honest Judge, cannot let a guilty person go free.

Now, here's the hinge question: Does it concern you, if you died today, that God would give you justice and find you guilty of breaking His moral law, the Ten Commandments?

Surely your answer is emphatically, YES!

I'm glad this is a concern to you. It concerns me as well. If you consider yourself to be a good person because of the good deeds you have done in your lifetime, think about this. How many GOOD DEEDS does it take to outweigh your BAD DEEDS? On the scale of God's justice, how much does each "good deed weigh" or how much does each "bad deed weigh?" Therefore, "good deeds vs. bad deeds" is not an accurate determination for entrance to Heaven.

Absolutely, no one should risk his eternity on such a dark gamble!

Now, the GOOD NEWS! *Romans 3:23 NKJV, "For all have sinned and fall short of the glory of God."* The only penalty that will satisfy the wrath of God or pay our sin debt is the death, burial, and resurrection of Jesus Christ. *John*

3:16 NJKV, "For God so loved the world that He gave His only begotten Son, that whoever believes in Him should not perish but have everlasting life." Romans 5:8 NKJV, "But God demonstrates His own love toward us, in that while we were still sinners, Christ died for us." The death, burial, and resurrection of Jesus Christ is not only an historical truth, it is also a spiritual truth. Jesus Christ saw you and me in serious trouble with God. He chose to take our place and suffer our death penalty on the cross. He was totally sinless but saw us as guilty before God, ready to be condemned to eternal flames of Hell. Jesus lovingly stepped up to die in our place.

His forgiveness is available- but is not automatic. Jesus does not merely love us the way we are. He loves us *in spite of* how we are. He loves us too much to leave us the way we are. (i.e. guilty sinners).

Now, more good news! Christ has made available the only way for anyone to enter Heaven. *John 14:6 NKJV, "Jesus said to him, 'I am the Way, the Truth, and the Life: no man comes to the Father, except through Me."* You can receive His free, gift of eternal life, by faith in His sacrifice on the cross of Calvary with repentance from sin.

Are you going to do this? When? Now?

Repentance is required along with faith in Jesus Christ alone-plus nothing else. Honest repentance is when we see our sin as seriously as God see it. We must confess with genuine sorrow. Not as in "sorry I got caught," but sorry that we have broken God's heart.

More good news! *Romans 10:9-10 NKJV, "That if you confess with your mouth the Lord Jesus, and believe in your heart that God has raised Him from the dead, you will be saved. For with the heart one believes unto righteousness; and with the mouth confession is made unto salvation."*

Honest repentance means; a change of our minds that changes our lives. We view sin differently. Sinful things we loved at one point in our lives, we now hate. Sinful things we had interest in, we now omit from our lives. We have a desire to please God. We want a pure relationship with Him!

When we have honestly repented, we are in a position to declare our faith in Jesus Christ. *Romans 10:13 NKJV, "For whoever calls on the name of the Lord shall be saved.*" To pray and declare you trust Him for your eternity in Heaven may be worded from your own heart. In the scripture when someone prayed for the gift of salvation, the sinner's prayer was short and straight to the point. Examples: Luke 18:13 NKJV, *"Lord, be merciful to me, a sinner."* Luke 23:42 *NKJV, "Then he said to Jesus, 'Lord, remember me when You come into Your kingdom.'"* Mark 9:24 *NKJV, "Lord, I believe. Help my unbelief."*

It is not a matter of saying the correct words. It is a matter of genuine, sincere, faith and repentance toward God.

This prayer results in a changed life. It is not a gradual process or journey. The Bible refers to this as "born again or salvation". A point in time event. Your way of thinking will change! It is not a process of trying to become a better person. It is an event where God forgives our sin and makes us His child, being born into a new family – the Family of God!

In each example that was mentioned, the sinner referred to God as "Lord", indicating surrender to His ownership. I encourage you to read the following scriptures:

John 3: 1-16 NKJV
There was a man of the Pharisees, named Nicodemus, a ruler of the Jews.
2 This man came to Jesus by night, and said to him, "Rabbi, we know that You are a teacher come from God; for no one can do these signs that You do, unless God is with him.
3 Jesus answered and said to him, "Most assuredly, I say to you, "Unless one is born again, he cannot see the kingdom of God."
4 Nicodemus said to him, "How can a man be born when he is old? Can he enter a second time into his mother's womb, and be born?
5 Jesus answered, "Most assuredly, I say to you, "Unless one is born of water and the Spirit, he cannot enter the kingdom of God.
6 That which is born of the flesh is flesh, that which is born of the Spirit is spirit.
7 Do not marvel that I said to you, 'You must be born again.'
8 The wind blows where it wishes, and you hear the sound of it, but cannot tell where it comes from and where it goes. So is everyone who is born of the Spirit.
9 Nicodemus answered and said to him, "How can these things be?"
10 Jesus answered and said to him, "Are you the teacher of Israel, and do not know these things?

11 *Most assuredly, I say to you, We speak what we know and testify what we have seen, and you do not receive Our witness.*

12 *If I have told you earthly things, and you do not believe, how will you believe, if I tell you heavenly things?*

13 *No one has ascended to heaven, but he who came down from heaven, that is, the Son of man who is in heaven.*

14 *And as Moses lifted up the serpent in the wilderness, even so must the Son of man be lifted up:*

15 *That whoever believes in him should not perish but have eternal life.*

16 *For God so loved the world, that He gave His only begotten Son, that whoever believes in Him should not perish, but have everlasting life.*

John 6: 28-29 NKJV

28 *Then they said to him, "What shall we do, that we may work the works of God?"*

29 *Jesus answered and said to them, "This is the work of God, that you believe in Him whom He sent."*

Acts 3: 19 NKJV

19 *Repent therefore, and be converted, that your sins may be blotted out, so that times of refreshing may come from the presence of the Lord.*

Acts 4: 12 NKJV

12 *"Nor is there salvation in any other, for there is no other name under heaven given among men, by which we must be saved."*

John 1: 12 NKJV

12 *But as many as received Him, to them He gave the right to become children of God, to those who believe in His name:*

Now that you have confessed and placed your faith in Jesus Christ, do any of the above scriptures relate or connect to your spirit? If so, continue to read:

John 10:28-29 NKJV

28 *And I give unto them eternal life, and they shall never perish neither shall any man snatch them out of my hand.*

29 *My Father, who has given them to me, is greater than all; and no one is able to snatch them out of my Father's hand.*

I John 5: 4 NKJV
4 You are of God, little children, and have overcome them, because He who is in you is greater that he who is in the world.

I John 3:2 NKJV
2 Beloved, now we are the children of God; and it has not yet been revealed what we shall be: but we know that, when He is revealed, we shall be like Him; for we shall see Him as He is.

I John 2: 12 – 16 NKJV
12 I write to you, little children, because your sins are forgiven you for His name's sake.
13 I write to you, fathers, because you have known Him who is from the beginning. I write to you, young men, because you have overcome the wicked one. I write to you, little children, because you have known the Father.
14 I have written to you, fathers, because you have known Him who is from the beginning. I have written to you, young men, because you are strong, and the word of God abides in you, and you have overcome the wicked one.
15 Do not love not the world, or the things in the world. If anyone loves the world, the love of the Father is not in him.
16 For all that is in the world, the lust of the flesh, the lust of the eyes, and the pride of life, is not of the Father, but is of the world."

I John 1:9 NKJV
9 If we confess our sins, He is faithful and just to forgive us our sins, and to cleanse us from all unrighteousness."

Romans 8: 1 NKJV
"There is therefore now no condemnation to those who are in Christ Jesus, who do not according to the flesh, but according to the Spirit."

II Corinthians 5:17 NJKV
17 Therefore, if anyone is in Christ, he is a new creation: old things have passed away; behold, all things have become new."

Power Questions and Action Points

1. Upon what are you basing your assurance of spending your eternity in Heaven?

2. Do you ever struggle with doubts about your salvation and your eternity?

3. Write out your experience of becoming a Christian. Does it line up with Romans 3:10, Romans 3:23, Romans 5:8, Romans 10:9-10, Romans 10:13, and John 3:16?

4. How often do you verbally share the good news of the gospel with other people?

5. Has your repentance of sin put you on an opposite direction in life?